400

# PREACHING
## THE MIRACLES OF JESUS

# PREACHING
# the MIRACLES
# of JESUS

by

Hillyer Hawthorne Straton, *1905-*

## ABINGDON-COKESBURY PRESS
### NEW YORK • NASHVILLE

# PREACHING THE MIRACLES OF JESUS

SET UP, PRINTED, AND BOUND BY THE PARTHENON PRESS, AT NASHVILLE, TENNESSEE, UNITED STATES OF AMERICA

*To my wife*

ALICE AVEN STRATON
who daily gives me
beauty, companionship, and inspiration

# Preface

MIRACLE stories occupy such a large place in the gospel narratives that to omit them in preaching is to leave out an essential part of the gospel message and to overlook a rich source of sermonic material; yet this is often what actually happens from a practical standpoint. Miracles are considered to be out-of-date and not the fashion in intellectual circles, so the use of miracle stories for preaching and teaching is quietly, though often unconsciously, avoided. Definite teaching values accompany the miracle accounts connected with the life of Jesus. In fact, the reason they were originally preserved was that early Christians found them helpful in their preaching and teaching ministry.

This book is intended to revive a knowledge and use of this wealth of material. My interest in the miracle stories grew out of my discovery of their value as preaching material. No claim is made here for extensive original scholarship. However, I have gone over the whole field carefully, and used the insights and wisdom of those who understand the Gospels much better than I. This volume endeavors to fill a definite need in the field of Christian literature by marshaling the main questions that have been raised about the gospel miracles. It frankly proceeds on the basis of a faith judgment, holding that miracles both can and did happen. Yet the critical questions concerning these stories have not been evaded. The emphasis has been upon the teaching and preaching values found in each account. An honest effort has been made to bring to the reader the pertinent facts in connection with each miracle. If there is any new contribution, it has grown out of the preaching and pastoral insights which a man discovers who endeavors to live close to people in their need.

The main divisions of the volume have a certain consistency.

Some students may feel that there is a rather arbitrary grouping within the divisions. With one or two exceptions, made necessary to include material traditionally considered a miracle, the reader will find that the chapters do hold together for purposes of preaching and teaching.

A typical instance of how the chapters can be of help is seen in Chapter 9, "Women Jesus Healed," where we have the three instances: the healing of Peter's mother-in-law, the straightening of the hunchbacked woman, and the curing of the woman who touched the hem of Jesus' garment. The accounts are separate and distinct. Each one of them can be used as an entity in itself. There is adequate material given for an intelligent study of each incident. However, the three accounts can very happily be tied together around the fact that Jesus had a real concern for those with no special station in the life of the times—in this case, women; in another, children; in still another, lepers.

I am under obligation to the wiser and better men than I who have devoted lifetimes to the study of the miracles. I particularly wish to acknowledge my debt to Professors Nels Ferré and Paul Minear, of Andover Newton Theological School, for reading portions of the manuscript and providing their critical judgment. Thanks are likewise due to Rev. Samuel Miller, of Cambridge, Massachusetts, who gave help at a number of places. I am indebted to Professor Henry Cadbury, of Harvard University, for his careful reading of the manuscript and his many helpful suggestions. His sympathetic understanding, genuine insights into the Scripture, and outstanding scholarship were an inspiration. This is true, though the positions adopted, in general and in each miracle, may or may not represent in any sense his views.

I wish, likewise, to thank my devoted wife, Alice Aven Straton, for her encouragement through the years and her help in proofreading; as well as my secretary, Mrs. F. Louise Carpenter, whose interest and ability in preparing the manuscript were of utmost assistance.

HILLYER HAWTHORNE STRATON

8

# Contents

## III. THE GREAT HEALER

CONTENTS

# IV. THE LIGHT OF THE WORLD

# V. THE DEFEATER OF DEMONS

# VI. THE GIVER OF LIFE

# 1

## Gospel Miracle and the Modern Temper

THE MODERN mechanistic world in which we live is one whose climate is singularly unresponsive to any and every account of miracle. The miracle stories connected with the life of Jesus are subject to this general atmosphere, along with the fantastic tales which are recorded of many ancient worthies. When miracles in the Gospels are considered, men in the pew would likely come under two broad classifications: first, those who accept the accounts uncritically, simply because they find them in the Bible; second, those whose educational background, based on a naturalistic position, plus what they consider to be a scientific understanding of the modern world, makes them skeptical of any such accounts on general principles. The Christian minister and other careful students of the Gospels who are aware of modern trends in biblical research and theological understanding find themselves in a dilemma. They, too, have been subject to the secularism of our present-day educational process, which tends to raise for them, as well as for the educated lay person, the same questions concerning miraculous accounts. However, the active layman and the minister of Jesus Christ with even short experience have discoverd in their contacts with life that factors do enter which cannot be explained by the ordinary processes of nature. Those who have had deep experience with prayer are aware of "a Power, not ourselves, that makes for righteousness."

The gospel miracles are connected with preaching and instruction. The form critics themselves would be the first to say

13

that we have the stories because they were found effective in the worship service of the early Christian circles. An interesting instance of this is in the recently discovered sermon of Melito on the Passion, in which he refers to John's account of the raising of Lazarus. In speaking about the Jewish rejection of Jesus, which was a very live subject in Melito's day (*ca.* A.D. 169-190), he says that they did not accept their Messiah: "Nor did the most marvelous sight of all abash thee, . . . a dead man buried in the tomb for four days, yet raised by him." [1]

When preaching the miracles of Jesus, the modern man of God must remember that men of the ancient world, with their limited and often very naïve view of nature, lived in what to us would be considered a fairyland. Anything that could not be explained by the ordinary course of events was neatly classified as a miracle. Heaven leaned low above the ancient world. People simply could not conceive of an earth without miracle.[2] The credulity of that day has to be reckoned with in studying the gospel miracles, even though one holds that New Testament miracles are in a category totally different from most of the fanciful tales of antiquity. The difference is due to the moral and spiritual values that are intimately associated with the various stories. Yet miracles in the gospel account are correctly subject to the same historical study as is accorded other parts of the gospel; and, as with other New Testament problems, the historical approach helps rather than hinders a true appreciation of all of the values in each account.

While biblical writers and church fathers did not hesitate to record or believe in miracle, they were often much more up-to-date than we sometimes give them credit for being. Augustine exhibits a strikingly modern viewpoint when he says that miracles are not contrary to nature; they are only contrary to nature so far as known by us.

[1] *Homily on the Passion* (Campbell Bonner, ed.), p. 177.
[2] See Shirley Jackson Case, *Experience with the Supernatural in Early Christian Times,* p. 3.

How is that contrary to nature which happens by the Will of God, since the Will of so mighty a Creator is certainly the nature of each created thing? A portent therefore happens not contrary to Nature, but contrary to what we know of Nature. [3]

God the Author and Creator of all Natures, does nothing contrary to Nature. . . . There is, however, no impropriety in saying that God does a thing contrary to Nature when it is contrary to what we know in Nature . . . but against the supreme law of Nature . . . God never acts, any more than He acts against Himself.[4]

Two strikingly contradictory positions of the age in which we live are its credulity from one standpoint and its blasé interrogative attitude from another. We are willing to accept the most improbable happening in the realm of the physical, especially if the word "science" is attached to it, whereas in the realm of faith all sorts of questions are raised about the simplest of propositions.

Physical wonders have ceased to amaze us, because we have seen so many things that once would have been characterized as miracles actually come to pass under our own eyes. Our generation has seen the birth and perfection of the airplane, the radio, and television. It has witnessed the dread fright of the release of atomic energy. Such wonders have accustomed us to believe that nothing is impossible in a scientific world.

A principal reason why gospel miracles have been quietly passed by both in the pastor's study and in the pulpit is the preconceived view that miracle and science are in conflict. If you add to this a false definition of miracle as a violation of all natural law, then Hume was probably right when he said that no amount of evidence would prove a miracle.[5] Our fathers were impressed by the apologetic value of miracle, but our generation has returned correctly to the true biblical position that miracles are primarily a demonstration of the power of God and his concern

[3] *De Civitate Dei* XXI. 8.
[4] *Contra Faustum* XXVI. 3.
[5] *An Inquiry Concerning the Human Understanding*, p. 114.

for working out his divine will for those who put their trust in him. They are only secondarily evidential in nature. Leading modern students of the subject, though they are sympathetic with the miracle concept, have abandoned the evidential value. William Adams Brown, who would be classified as among the most forward-looking Christian scholars and statesmen of our day, put it succinctly, "The miracle as apologetic has gone—the concept of miracle has not." [6]

When our forefathers believed in miracle, they were believing that God ruled and that he was present and active in his world. Whatever we may believe about one particular miracle, if we give up this great fact, we do so at our own peril. Incidentally, this is the position taken by nearly all competent recent students of the problem. They may vary as to their approach, but they hold this in common. One modern theologian says, "We must see to it that we retain the core of truth: the reality of God's activity in the world as direct and vital and the unpredictable element in life, which makes it ever fresh and new, although never merely strange and inexplicable." [7]

It must be strongly emphasized that miracle in the modern usage, and in a true biblical sense, is not a violation of law.[8] While the biblical writers did not have our modern concept of law, they did have a philosophy of nature which involved the belief that all natural phenomena were subject to the power and control of God. It has been pointed out by keen scientific and theological students of the subject that our understanding of natural law is so limited that we are rash to say that any event violates it. Some of the most careful and thoughtful modern scientists are recognizing that we do not live in a closed mechanis-

[6] "Permanent Significance of Miracle for Religion," *Harvard Theological Review*, July, 1915, p. 300.

[7] W. N. Pittenger, *The Christian Way in a Modern World*, p. 69.

[8] With the finest of philosophical and Christian insight C. S. Lewis, in his book *Miracles*, strengthens this whole position. His work is a "must" book for those who would adequately study the subject. It is especially helpful as a background for this volume.

tic system. Ours is a world where the insight of Jesus is as profound as when he first uttered it, "My Father worketh hitherto, and I work." Science today teaches that nature is plastic to internal forces. F. R. Tennant has well asked the question, "Then why should it not be likewise plastic to forces from without?" [9]

The fact that we are able to account for a miracle by a natural explanation in no sense involves the surrender of the belief in miracle. *If God enters the situation, the miracle is still there.* In fact, the truest understanding of biblical miracle is right at this point. The record says that when the Israelites crossed the Red Sea, God caused a strong east wind to blow, thereby giving us the method employed. The miracle does not consist in a wonder contrary to all experience or possibility, but in the fact that God enters the situation when necessary to carry out his holy will. All human experience teaches that the universe is not only rational but also moral. The supernatural can still be believed when natural explanations are adduced. [10]

There have been almost as many definitions of miracle as persons who have thought at all seriously about it. Radicals have defined miracle in such a manner as to prejudice the case according to their views. Without falling into this pit, can we form a modern definition of miracle that is true to what science has observed, what the best of religious intelligence feels to be true, and what the Bible reveals? Our answer is: A miracle demonstrates God's concern for carrying out his holy will, employing methods in keeping with his power, his wisdom, and his love to work out for men moral and spiritual ends.

There are laws in the natural world which we are able to classify. Logic induces us to believe that there are likewise laws in the spiritual world and that miracle itself is subject to law—that there is a law of miracle. The Bible certainly implies that

[9] *Miracle and Its Philosophical Presuppositions*, p. 47.

[10] George J. Romanes, *Thoughts on Religion*, pp. 119-21. "It is no argument against the divine origin of a thing or event to prove it due to natural causation."

such is the case, and that prayer and faith are part and parcel of the law of miracle.[11] In preaching on the miracles to a modern congregation, the minister who points out some possible scientific explanation for an account will notice a marked ripple of favorable response through the congregation. Here is an indication of the scientific attitude of our day plus the unwillingness on the part of religious people to give up the actuality of the event.

The problem ultimately revolves itself around a philosophy of the natural and the supernatural. If "naturalism" is defined as ruling God out of his universe and supernaturalism is defined as God's coming into the universe in utterly extraordinary and arbitrary ways, then we have a tension which is unresolvable.

In the field of Christian thought there is a return today to a vital supernaturalism which is bound up in God's personal relation to men and is seen particularly in the birth, the life, the death, and the resurrection of Jesus of Nazareth. The leaders in this movement in Christian circles have been aptly termed biblical realists. They have held to a high and holy supernaturalism often tinged with mysticism. It is a supernaturalism based on the understanding of God as personal. God acts as we expect one person to act in his relation with another. It cannot be explained. It is like love—it has to be felt, and it is felt, in terms of a God who really sent his Son into the world that the world through him might be saved.

Men in the twentieth century find difficulty with the gospel miracles because of a "reporter" type of mind. If the Fourth Evangelist were asked about the factualness of his account, he would likely respond, "Of course the events are true. Did not Jesus show by his life, words, deeds, and resurrection that he was all-powerful?" The difference between his attitude and ours is that we are using our standards of factual exactness to weigh a first-century judgment as to whole truth. Ought not our chief

[11] Documenting this statement would involve a reference to nearly every miracle in the Bible. Two are sufficient: Before crossing the Red Sea, Moses "cried unto the Lord." Jesus "did not many mighty works there *because of their unbelief.*"

concern to be with the over-all truth of the Gospels, of which the miracle stories are a very definite part?

One factor must never be forgotten, and that is that history is more than a chronicle of facts. It is an interpretation of events as well, and the interpretation is essential to give the total picture of a situation. Simply to record a fact without putting it into its historical locale as to time and place is often to do violence to the fact. A bare chronicle of the storming of the Bastille or the abdication of Edward VIII as king of England for "the woman I love" does not give the true picture. The events are of such a character that the meaning of what took place is of far greater significance, historically speaking, than what actually happened. The evangelists were not historians in our modern sense. They were concerned with giving us simply those factors necessary to understand who Jesus is. If we had a bare chronicle of events and even sayings of Jesus, without interpretation, we would not have true history.

Henry Cadbury, in his recent fine study, *Jesus: What Manner of Man*, points out that the teachings of Jesus may not have been the factor of greatest novelty, but that his hearers believed his words were given authority by his miracles. "Believe me for the very works' sake." He says:

> Jesus' teaching gained prestige from his miracles. There can be little doubt of that. . . . There is no evidence that Jesus' contemporaries would limit the power to work miracles to the Messiah. Yet a Messiah without miracles, even a prophet without miracles, may have seemed to them unlikely. [12]

The men who were closest to Jesus believed in his power to work miracles. That the disciples were not completely naïve is seen by the fact that they did not believe John the Baptist worked miracles.[13]

[12] P. 111.

[13] John 10:41. The view that the author of the Fourth Gospel wants to picture Jesus in sharp contrast to John the Baptist and hence makes such a statement has to be reckoned with, yet it must still be remembered that the Synoptic Gospels record no miracles by John the Baptist.

A large group of miracles today are readily and almost universally accepted by all schools of thought, including those of the most liberal. These are largely miracles of healing, for which we can give a rationale in modern terms. There are other gospel accounts which are acknowledged by many students to be coincidences, though they were remembered and described as miracles. Such might be the stilling of the storm and the healing of the Gerasene demoniac. Today the most exact and scientific of us still use the language of appearance, saying, "The sun rises." The Bible likewise speaks in this fashion. This gives reason to accept other miracle accounts. It would be held that they were not so marvelous as they were believed to be.[14] Such an incident could be the raising of Jairus' daughter, for here Jesus himself said that she was not dead, and it is possible that he meant this literally.

There are a small number of miracles which become the crux of the historical problem. Among these would be the accounts of the stilling of the tempest, feeding of the five thousand, walking on the sea, and the raising of Lazarus. These would generally be disbelieved by advanced thinkers, and yet a very respectable group of biblical scholars continue to hold to some or all of them, though they might not be able to explain them. For instance, C. H. Dodd might question from a critical standpoint any one of the nature miracles on what he considered valid ground from an internal critical standpoint. Yet in speaking of such accounts he says, "The judgment that the healing and exorcisms are nonmiraculous and historical and the nature miracles legendary is not warranted by any difference in the attestation of the two types of miracle story." [15]

Our inability at the present time to know how a certain sign —or to use the less accurate translation, "miracle"—might have been accomplished becomes decisive. Our scientific age demands

[14] See Brown, *op. cit.*, p. 308. "Miracle belief is often due to lack of knowledge."
[15] *Expository Times*, Aug., 1933.

a *modus operandi;* and if this can be furnished, the problem is solved for large groups of thinkers. Those who disbelieve the gospel miracles do so on the a priori theory of a certain observed uniformity of nature, a philosophy in this realm of "it can't happen here." Those who believe the miracle accounts do so on the theological theory of the possibility and actuality of divine intervention by a personal God when moral or spiritual ends are to be accomplished. It must be recognized that presuppositions are ultimately involved in either instance.

Whatever presuppositions exist in the present study—and I trust I have held them to a minimum—are based on the second of the above two positions. The expositions of the various miracles of Jesus which follow are based upon the assumption of their validity. We may as well recognize that there is no ultimate rationale that will explain or account for what we call miracle. Compare almost any gospel miracle with the modern wonder of radar, which enables us to see through fog or night. One is scarcely more marvelous than the other. Though we know much about electronics, the ultimate nature of electrical energy that makes this modern miracle possible is hidden from our understanding. We use radar to bring ships safely into port, though we may not understand in the last analysis how it operates. As with many of the greatest facts and truths of life, miracle ultimately cannot be explained. It can best be felt and described.

# 2

## Gospel Miracle and Faith

MIRACLE, like faith, has its own category of reality. Essential Christian faith has a vital bearing for thoughtful students of the whole problem. At the heart of this essential Christian belief are three elements of ultimate discontinuity. None of them can finally be explained or accounted for save on the basis of faith. They are (1) redemption, (2) the resurrection of Jesus, (3) immortality.

The first does have some elements which the psychologists say are explainable, and yet the whole Christian thesis that a Man on a cross provides redemption for all who will believe on him is in the realm of faith. Great thinkers have spent a lifetime, weighty tomes have been written endeavoring to make plain the how and why of redemption, but the fact remains that it cannot be explained. Ultimately we do not know how "the blood of Jesus Christ his son cleanseth us from all sin," but practically we have experienced this cleansing, and so we believe in it. We know it is true.

The resurrection of Jesus is the second cardinal Christian belief. Whatever may be our theories of what took place, Christians everywhere and under all circumstances acknowledge that Christ "was raised on the third day in accordance with the scriptures." This, too, is in the realm of discontinuity. The ancient thinker asked, "How are the dead raised up? and with what body do they come?" The answer today is the same answer that Paul gave, "It is sown a natural body; it is raised a spiritual

22

GOSPEL MIRACLE AND FAITH

body." We cannot explain the resurrection. We can only describe it and show what faith in the resurrection has done for them that believe.

The third essential Christian belief is that of immortality, and it also involves the matter of faith. From a narrowly scientific viewpoint it too represents what we might call discontinuity. When year after year, century after century, the best of men look upon the forms of their dead and then when they likewise die, it seems that the ancient observer was right, "As it happeneth to the fool, so it happeneth even to me; and why was I then more wise?"

Death seems so utterly final. The dead do not come back. We do not hear from them again. It is the end. All of our experience tells us that it is the end. Dust goes unto dust. For a little while we have the spark of life, of hope, of dreams, but it is lost in silence, buried in vastness, drowned in the depths of utter blankness. This is what we observe, yet the Christian dares to assume that this is not the answer, that man does live after death. He believes in the life everlasting. Here, as with the resurrection of Jesus, there is a leap of faith. If we believe in immortality, so far as all human judgments are concerned, we believe in discontinuity. We believe that God enters the situation for moral and spiritual ends and that death as we know it is not the final answer, but that the visions, expectations, and the high hopes of men at their noblest are true.

There is an observable progression here. Redemption shows discontinuity. We cannot ultimately account for it, but looking about us we see countless evidences of redemption. We know people who are born again. We observe the radically bad man changed into the radically good man. Although we cannot account for redemption, we know it is a fact, for we can observe many of our friends and acquaintances who have been redeemed.

The resurrection of Jesus can no more be accounted for in its final essence than can redemption. The whole weight of New Testament evidence supports the record of the resurrection of

Jesus with such a powerful witness that the most careful and exact scholars admit that there was some extraordinary phenomenon which took place. They readily say that it can be best explained in such terms as are used by the New Testament writers. The very existence of the Christian Church is one of the greatest of the buttresses to belief in the resurrection, and is recognized as such. Psychologically you cannot account for the Church apart from belief in the resurrection of Jesus. Along with the fact of the Church we have the gospel records saying that Jesus appeared to the disciples on numerous occasions. Paul refers to more than five hundred who saw the risen Lord. Other New Testament writers are as certain of it as was Paul. The Christian Church was founded on this faith. These are the facts. At the same time everyday experience tells us that it could not have happened and that it did not happen. But theistic and Christian experience tells us at the same time that the resurrection of Jesus is not contrary to what God can and will do. Because of the evidence we have, *we do believe that it did happen*, that Jesus is "risen from the dead, and become the firstfruits of them that slept." From an objective, evidential standpoint there is less proof for the resurrection of Jesus than there is for redemption.

The matter of immortality is wholly subjective, completely in the realm of faith. We lay our dead away, and that is the end so far as any objective confirmation is concerned. Christian faith steps in here, as it does with the question of redemption and the resurrection of Jesus, and says, "Because he lives, we too shall live." Immortality is at the very heart of our Christian faith. It cannot be explained; it simply is believed. It is the essence of Christian faith and is based ultimately on the goodness and the concern of a personal God who wills that not any of his children should perish, but that we might all find the fullness of being as it is in him.

The above is not irrelevant to our consideration of the problem of miracle. It is at the center of it. If by faith we believe in redemption, in the resurrection of Jesus, and in our own resurrection, we have already taken the leap of faith. The question of the possibility of miracle should be settled for us. God intervened at the time of the death of his own Son on the cross, and so Jesus was raised from the dead. God intervenes at the time of our redemption through faith in his Son Jesus Christ and gives us newness of life. God will intervene at our own death to usher us into the place "prepared for them that love him," where "his servants shall serve him." God intervenes because in each instance moral and spiritual ends are to be accomplished. The modern Christian therefore is not out of step with reality and with faith when he believes in miracle. He is more completely in step with them.

The innermost core of the whole problem is our understanding of the personality of Jesus of Nazareth. If God spoke through the unique life of goodness and wisdom of his Son for the redemption of mankind, then the one in whose face we see the glory of God *did* work miracles. He believed that his power was from God; his disciples believed it; his enemies had to account for it and did so by blasphemous accusation that he was in league with the devil.

The New Testament, rather than being a wonder book, is singularly free from miracle accounts when the total picture is considered. The Gospels are unanimous in referring to numerous miracles which Jesus wrought, but for the most part only typical cases are recorded. The evangelists "practiced a remarkable reserve in their reports." [1] If the Gospels were simply a collection of marvels, the temptation to record such stories of John the Baptist would have been almost irresistible.

There are about thirty-five miracles recorded in the Gospels. In a number of instances Jesus is referred to as performing mighty works which have no further description. "They brought unto him many that were possessed with devils: and he cast out the spirits with his word, and healed all that were sick." (Matt. 8:16; see also Mark 1:32-34, Luke 4:40-41.) "Jesus went about

---

[1] Edwin Lewis in the *Abingdon Bible Commentary*, p. 922.

. . . healing every sickness and every disease." (Matt. 9:35.) These mighty works are often interpreted in our common translation by the word "miracle." He was considered by his contemporaries to possess remarkable powers, and he himself shared unquestionably in this view. "My Father worketh hitherto, and I work." (John 5:17.) "Woe to you, Chorazin! . . . for if the mighty works done in you had been done in Tyre and Sidon, they would have repented long ago in sackcloth and ashes." (Matt. 11:21 R.S.V.) His disciples believed he had remarkable power, and his enemies admitted it. Whatever Jesus may have thought about his own mighty works, it is evident that he meant "miracle," or else he could not have condemned the city for unbelief. The evidence is plain that Jesus believed he had accomplished things of sufficient moment to give reason for repentance. Jesus felt that he had the power to heal, and the record is clear that he healed on every occasion except when there was a lack of faith or when the request was simply for a magical demonstration.

This leads us to a consideration of the New Testament term which is commonly translated by the word "miracle" in English and *Wunder* in German. Both are most unfortunate translations because in the twentieth century they carry a connotation of magic, impossibility, and even abnormality which the four words [2] in the Gospels that they translate do not necessarily connote. Archbishop Trench pointed this out nearly ninety years ago. The recent revision committee recognized this and did not use the word "miracle" in the new Revised Standard Version of the New Testament. With the gospel writers it is never a case of impossibility, for "with God all things are possible." Jesus regarded his signs and mighty works as an evidence that the

[2] The four words used to translate "miracles" are: τέρατα (wonders), σημεῖα (signs), δυνάμεις (powers), and ἔργα (works). The word "wonder," which comes closer to our word "miracle," is never used alone; it is "signs and wonders." If our common versions had always translated "miracle" with some qualifying word—possibly "miracle signs"—the impression of magical impossibility would not be as strong.

Kingdom of God was at hand. The working of miracles was expected of the Messiah.

The principal significance of the miracles is bound up with the fact that they belong to the new age Jesus came to institute. Long ago Seeley wrote that the most marvelous thing about the miracles of Jesus was the mighty powers "which he held under a mighty control, never employing them for himself." [3] Jesus constantly refused to work miracles as demonstrations for their own sakes before those who would not understand them. "A wicked and adulterous generation seeketh after a sign; and there shall be no sign given unto it, but the sign of the prophet Jonas." (Matt. 16:4.) The reserve of Jesus in this connection is especially significant, for the record is plain that he was conscious of power from God to bring blessing and help when needed. His mighty works are a part of the general proclamation of the Kingdom of God.

Jesus believed that the power which he possessed was from God. His works were delegated power. In the passage where he is accused by his enemies of casting out devils by Beelzebub, Jesus gives the source of his power. "But if it is by the finger of God that I cast out demons, then the kingdom of God has come upon you." (Luke 11:20 R.S.V.) In most instances prayer accompanied the work. In fact, the whole problem of miracle is bound up with the problem of petitionary prayer. Jesus had supreme faith in the efficacy of prayer; had he not said "men ought always to pray" and given his disciples the world's model prayer? His faith that his heavenly Father would hear his prayer was unshaken, for he was the ideal Son, the founder of the new order.

In the Synoptic Gospels, Jesus rejects the role of wonder worker, as just noted. Yet he never turns away genuine human need; "I will; be thou clean" echoes through his public ministry. The element of compassion in this ministry is large. The miracles

[3] *Ecce Homo*, Chap. 5.

have been called, with some insight, Christ's method of philanthropy. The recognition that he has power from his Father and that as the Messiah he should exercise it to show the supremacy of the Kingdom of God over the kingdom of Satan is a motivating factor in his mighty works. The evidential character is there also, but it is a by-product rather than a prime cause. Chorazin ought to have repented, but he would no more have "passed a miracle" there for this purpose alone than he would have leaped from the temple pinnacle to gain the plaudits of the Jerusalem mob. He carefully avoided the spectacular in connection with his works. In still other towns the lack of faith completely tied his hands; "he did not many mighty works there because of their unbelief." Prayer and faith were the two inevitable and necessary prerequisites to the release of divine power through Jesus. He recognized clearly that "mighty works" alone would not be sufficient to convince those who cared not to believe. "Neither will they be persuaded, though one rose from the dead" is his comment at the close of the parable of Lazarus and Dives.

In John the evidential nature of miracle is given greater prominence. However, many writers have greatly exaggerated it. It is unscientific to say that John is interested only in the marvelous and the mighty. He has no reference to cures of demoniacs. John does not give new reasons for telling miracle stories. They are signs of genuine spiritual significance for him as well as for the writers of the Synoptic Gospels. In contrast to the other evangelists John often has a long discourse intimately connected with the miracle account and growing out of it. This is a typical Johannine stylistic method. We expect and find more theological reflection in John's Gospel than in the others. However, all four Gospels give evidence of theological connection with their miracle accounts, as for instance the condemnation of Chorazin for not believing.

As pointed out above, Jesus is constantly depicted in the Gospels as more interested in opening spiritually blind eyes, unstopping spiritually deaf ears, and raising the spiritually dead, than in performing the physical mighty works recorded of him. Yet "the miracle of his acts was not that they were manifestations of omnipotent power, but that they were manifestations of omnipotent love." [4] In the Synoptic Gospels and in John, Jesus is persuaded that he has power from his heavenly Father "to work the works of him that sent me." For the purposes of faith, as well as this volume, we will endeavor to look at the miracles as did the evangelists, who saw in them a living, visible manifestation of the love and power of God which they witnessed in Jesus of Nazareth. It is Jesus himself who is the supreme miracle; and once we have grasped this great truth, the account of his signs, works, and powers will have such a transforming effect in our lives that we too will fulfill his prophecy, "Greater works than these shall he do; because I go unto my Father."

Prayer and faith must accompany miracles. They are deeds of compassion; they are deeds of mercy; they are signs of the coming of the kingdom.

[4] C. J. Wright, *Miracle in History and in Modern Thought*, p. 323.

# 3

## Water into Wine

THE STORY of Jesus' turning the water into wine in John 2:1-11 is followed by remarks of the evangelist,[1] "This beginning of miracles did Jesus in Cana of Galilee, and manifested forth his glory." Christians can well thank the author for the use of the words, "this beginning of miracles did Jesus." How easily a new public figure or a new regime is characterized and typed. The audience began to laugh before the late Will Rogers said a word. A congregation of Baptists in the Southland would take out their handkerchiefs and start to wipe their eyes before the deeply loved southern preacher George Truett uttered a single phrase. When La Guardia became mayor of New York City, he immediately started to work twelve hours a day. This was in marked contrast to his predecessor, Jimmie Walker, who

---

[1] It is beyond the scope of this work to consider the problems of Johannine authorship, but the position which holds that the apostle John is the source behind most of the material in the Fourth Gospel, while not the major view in scholarly circles, does have the advantage of solving more of the admitted problems than any other. Whether the Gospel was put into its present shape by "the Witness" or "John, the presbyter" is really of little more moment than Mark's use of the preaching of Peter as his main source; a valid authority is behind both works.

The last word is yet to be said on the Johannine problem. Interesting facts and monographs which throw new light on the subject are appearing regularly. A. T. Olmstead, in his *Jesus in the Light of History*, makes the amazing claim that John was the first Gospel written, not the last. He dates it about A.D. 40. See also F. R. Goodenough, "John, a Primitive Gospel," *Journal of Biblical Literature*, June, 1945; likewise my article, "What Jesus Thought About Himself," *Christendom*, Spring, 1945. See also footnote on p. 164.

rarely got down to his office before two P.M. The new regime was thus very early typed, and the results of this characterization were evidenced in every department of the city government.

Martin Dibelius says this story is of extra-Christian origin and classifies it as a "tale," having a possible connection with Dionysus [2] or some god of wine—a story which was transferred to Jesus, of all people! Dibelius too lightly brushes it aside as having "nothing at all to do with the Gospel ethos." This is an amazing illustration of how a scholar can completely miss a truth that is even exceptionally compatible with our modern ways of thinking.

R. H. Strachan, in contrast to Dibelius, has an attitude toward this story that is well to keep in mind:

In our approach to this story we ought not first to concern ourselves with the general question of the supernatural. The Evangelist found the basis of this story in the traditional records of the ministry of Jesus, and selects it for his own purpose. To him, it is an instrument to convey the truth that *Jesus manifested his glory and his disciples believed on him.* It is profitless to attempt to "rationalize" such stories. Whatever its origin, it must be assumed that the Evangelist regards the story as describing an actual occurrence. He found in it a rich means of expression in symbol of the course of Christ's ministry, now about to be inaugurated.[3]

Of the farfetched Dionysian source C. J. Wright says:

The theory is interesting, but, to the present writer, it is fanciful to suppose that the Evangelist was here influenced by such legends. The symbolism of wine was widespread, and it is much more likely that the Hebrew Christian who wrote this Gospel was using a familiar metaphor used by Jesus, and some incident in his Ministry, and that from these two sources he had written the parable before us. [4]

[2] A familiar Greek legend has Dionysus producing wine on certain annual occasions. See Edwyn Hoskyns, *The Fourth Gospel*, I, 199-200; Euripides *Bacchae*. 704-5; J. Estlin Carpenter, *The Johannine Writings*, p. 380.

[3] *The Fourth Gospel*, p. 122.

[4] H. D. A. Major, T. W. Manson, and C. J. Wright, *The Mission and Message of Jesus*, p. 726. Wright's comment here is pertinent even though he believes the account is to be understood allegorically.

There is an artlessness about the combination of the human and the divine in John that gives us reason to believe there was such a fusion in real life. The evangelist tells us he is writing to "manifest the glory" of Jesus. Would he ever have selected a homely peasant wedding party for this purpose had there been no basis in fact?

The account shows us an insight into the very heart of the Master and his desire to bring abundant life to men. Without specially intending to do so, John gives us the same picture we have in the Synoptic Gospels of Jesus as a man among men, a friend of the lowly, one who so rejoiced to be with people at dinner that he could be called a "gluttonous man, and a wine-bibber" (Luke 7:34) by smallhearted men who could not comprehend the greatness of his personality. Such factors have a peculiar appeal for our day. Yet we must remember that such side lights upon character were incidental to the author's main purpose of stressing the symbolism of the need for the purification of Judaism (vs. 6) and its transformation by Christ into the wine of eternal life. "The law was given by Moses, but grace and truth came by Jesus Christ." (John 1:17.) The very identical nature of these character presentations makes them all the more revealing.

The modern wants to know, "Is it true? Did the incident really happen?" The evangelist would never have thought of asking the question. He passed on the story as he received it, or recalled its benediction after a lifetime of rich reflection. "He no doubt intends his narrative to be accepted as at any rate approximately true history," says Macgregor.[5] Bernard writes, "The way in which the story is told goes far to support the view that it is a genuine reminiscence." [6] Our main concern today is with the factual reality of the account, but the evan-

[5] *The Gospel of John* ("Moffatt New Testament Commentary"), p. 55.
[6] *The Gospel According to St. John* ("International Critical Commentary"), p. 80.

gelist was concerned with the deeply symbolic value of this story as one of the seven miracles he records.

The ministry of Jesus was inevitably given a certain tone by his first words and his first deeds. Note the infancy wonder stories that have come down to us. In one the boy Jesus has been playing with clay, making mud pies and clay pigeons. He claps his hands together over a clay pigeon. It comes to life and flies away. In another, a child who has displeased the boy Jesus is struck dead by a glance of his eye. These words of John, "This beginning of miracles," along with Luke's account of the boy-hood of Jesus (Luke 2:41-52) assure us that Jesus was a normal person who grew as any other normal person has to grow. When the great prophet Moses appeared before Pharaoh in his first miracle, water was turned into blood. When Jesus began his public ministry, water was changed into the wine of gladness. A greater than Moses came to bless men, not curse them. Whether consciously in this case or not, Jesus on more than one occasion set himself in contrast to Moses. Jesus did not come primarily to feed five thousand people or provide wine for weddings, but both acts do symbolize his mission of blessings for mankind. This miracle, so intimately connected with the traditional wedding ceremony, is probably more familiar than any other. There is a benediction in its sacred connection with one of the holy moments of life.

In the temptation experience, which must have shortly preceded the wedding at Cana, Jesus was tempted to turn stones into bread. Satan very probably endeavored to sell Jesus on the necessity for using his power to strengthen his own body. From the temptation experience right through his whole public ministry, Jesus steadfastly refused to use his miraculous power for his own benefit. His mighty power held under mighty control was for the blessing of men, whether at a wedding of gladness or with a throng who needed healing.

Jesus' ministry was contrasted, not only with that of Moses, but also with that of his more immediate predecessor, John the

Baptist. A thundering prophet, ascetic and austere, John the Baptist would not have been at a wedding in the first place. If he was a Nazarite, which is entirely probable, he certainly would not have partaken of wine or provided it for others. Prophets have their place, and John was among the greatest,[7] but they have been more noted for denunciation and exposé than for service to others. No less than John, Jesus was a lover of righteousness, yet he came as a brother and a friend of men, to dine with them in their homes, to rejoice with them at their weddings, to weep with them in their sorrow.

The popular expectation was that the Messiah as the Son of man would appear riding the clouds in royal splendor and coming out of the sea. It was as familiar to Jesus as the average Jew of his day. Our Lord came to do completely the will of his Father. Jesus had an intuitive knowledge that his mission was not to frown on mirth or apocalyptically bring life to a close. He was to fulfill life by participating in fellowship with the people of his day. In the process if the popular conception of the Messiah needed to be changed, then let it be changed. "Bridegroom" was a term Jesus employed on several occasions. The "joy of the bridegroom" served as a metaphor of blessing that was appropriately a part of his mission to bring life, and that abundantly.

Is the statement of the evangelist that a wedding showed forth his glory incongruous? This was no *Ostentationswunder*. Jesus did not here "pass a miracle" simply to convince the disciples of his power. This is one of those human touches that so endear Jesus to us. It was like his call to little children to come unto him. "Forbid them not, to come unto me: for of such is the kingdom of heaven." Jesus is one with us. He is not a distant, incomprehensible Messiah, but the friend and the brother of mankind. Jesus not only turned water into wine, but he enjoyed a wedding. In our sophisticated day a wedding is the one thing people

[7] According to Jesus, Matt. 11:8-11.

will still go out of their way to attend. From that day to this every Christian wedding has referred, with a sense of gladness, to that event when Jesus was present on a similar occasion.

The Eastern wedding festival was a time of unusual rejoicing.[8] It provided a break in the otherwise drab lives of the people. Oil and wine were distributed to adults, and nuts and dried fruit to the children. It was a time of gladness almost comparable to our Christmas. On the appointed evening the bride was led with music to the home of the bridegroom. There was a gay and colorful procession with lamps, torches, and flowers carried by the members of the bridal party.[9] Passers-by either joined the procession or saluted it. It was customary to praise the beauty and the virtue of the bride as she journeyed to the home of the bridegroom.

We find Jesus at the wedding with a number of his disciples, who possibly included John, James, Philip, and Nathanael. According to legend, John the son of Zebedee was the bridegroom. Even if this is pure fantasy, John and James were likely present. Cana was the home of Nathanael (John 21:2), and Jesus had asked Philip (John 1:43) to go with him to Galilee. The story of the intervention of Jesus on the plea of his mother leads us to believe that he was a relative of either the bride or the groom. The bridegroom was under no obligation to invite the disciples as well as the rabbi. Here is an evidence of the groom's largehearted and spontaneous nature. It may account, in part, for the shortage of refreshments. Failure to provide enough wine may have been due to poverty or the generosity of the bridegroom, who wanted everyone in the vicinity to share his joy. Thinking of the incident in later years the bridegroom surely recalled with a sense of blessing the fact that Jesus was there to grace his wedding day.

Most weddings in Christian lands at least give lip service to the faith Jesus founded. The divorce rate would be far lower if

---

[8] See Alfred Edersheim, *The Life and Times of Jesus the Messiah*, Chap. 4.
[9] See Jesus' description in the parable of the ten virgins (Matt. 25:1-13).

Jesus' ideal of the sacredness of human personality and his in-grained respect for womanhood were the ideals of every husband—and yes, every wife as well. In marriage man and woman join hands with God as they join their bodies in creative impulse. "My Father worketh hitherto," said Jesus. Creation is continuous, and men have a sacramental part in its mystery. The "twain shall be one flesh." (Matt. 19:5.) "Moses because of the hardness of your hearts [permitted divorce]: but from the beginning it was not so." (Matt. 19:8.) "God made them male and female. . . . For this cause shall a man leave his father and mother, and cleave to his wife." (Mark 10:6-7).

Jesus brings a benediction to this most joyful of all human ceremonies in far more significant fashion than the flowers about the altar or the "Wedding March" from *Lohengrin*. The procession of the bride in the whiteness of all her glory reminds us that Jesus referred to himself as the bridegroom (Matt. 9:15). Calling the Church the bride of Christ is a simile of rare beauty.

The little town of Cana was not far from Nazareth. As a kins-woman, Mary the mother of Jesus may have had a special obligation in connection with this particular wedding. Her concern about food and drink, plus her actions, shows that she was close enough to the household to feel free to give directions to the servants. When Mary came to Jesus with the words "They have no wine," she was uttering a simple statement of need. Jesus would be interested, for he too was a kinsman. Though the disciples were invited, it was largely an event within a family circle.[10] As the evangelist specifically claims that this was the beginning of Jesus' miracles, it is extremely doubtful that Mary expected anything unusual. Mary might have thought that Jesus, as a rabbi returning to Galilee with a group of disciples, would prove himself gracious by sending out for more wine. Bengel makes an interesting suggestion when he says that this was a

[10] Augustus Strong gives this as the reason the incident was unknown to the other evangelists, or seemingly outside the range of Jesus' official ministry (*Addresses on the Gospel of John*, p. 64).

broad hint from Mary to her Son that it would be advisable for him and his disciples to leave![11] This would break up the wedding party before the embarrassment of the shortage of wine was discovered. John Calvin conjectured that Mary wanted Jesus to make a speech and thereby relieve the situation![12]

The reply of Jesus, "Woman, what have you to do with me?[13] My hour has not yet come,"[14] conveys two false impressions today. The first, that Jesus was rude to his mother; the second, that he was looking forward to his passion. The first part of the statement was in no sense harsh. Remember that Jesus used somewhat the same expression to his mother when he was commending her to the care of the apostle John at the time of the crucifixion. "Woman, behold thy son." A good modern translation is "Lady." The southern expression "Yes, ma'm" of a dutiful son to his mother is even a better rendition. At the beginning of the public ministry the evangelist has Jesus assert to his mother a new relation. The early synoptic gospel passage where Jesus calls himself "the bridegroom" (Mark 2:19-20) is an oblique messianic reference for those "who have eyes to see." It is some indication that John's statement is not a product wholly of meditation in retrospect. "The bride" is a figure the early Christians immediately adopted.

Paul makes telling use of the symbol of the bride and the bridegroom. "Husbands, love your wives, even as Christ also loved the church, and gave himself for it; . . . That he might present it to himself a glorious church, not having spot or wrinkle, or any such thing; but that it should be holy and without blemish." (Eph. 5:25, 27.)

As the wedding for both the bridegroom and the bride is the

[11] Richard C. Trench, *Notes on the Miracles of Our Lord*, p. 87.

[12] William M. Taylor, *Miracles of Our Savior*, p. 32.

[13] Τί ἐμοὶ καὶ σοί.

[14] Revised Standard Version. There has been much discussion about the meaning of the words. The evident difficulty in this statement, plus the problem raised by the rather crude jest of the master of ceremonies, is a mark of genuineness for the whole account. Fictional stories avoid difficulties.

sign of full maturity—life truly beginning for both as they lose themselves in each other—so it is with the coming of the Messiah, the "bridegroom," in the fullness of time. The Kingdom of God is at hand; now life can truly begin for the people of God. In keeping with the metaphor the "bride," the people of God, henceforth does not lead her own life; all depends on the "bridegroom." Whenever the Church as the "bride" has held high the consciousness of her central loyalty to Christ, the "bridegroom," she has been spotless and strong and a blessing to all.

This passage early in Mark is evidence of messianic consciousness hinted to his disciples long before the disclosure at Caesarea-Philippi. The question "What have you to do with me?" is not a rebuke, but a suggestion of misunderstanding from a dutiful son. As a very wise son Jesus knew that the time comes when the child must live for himself. Parents do a disservice to children when they bind them to their apron strings. Jesus was no longer merely Mary's son or the groom's kinsman; now he belonged to the world, certainly so in his own mind. He was to show his responsibility to the world by providing for human need. However, this responsibility was not on the basis of kinship, but of service. The last part, "My hour is not yet come," simply means that it is not time for Jesus to intervene. Those who contend that it is a reference to the Passion should remember that according to John's chronology it was at least three years to the time of his crucifixion.[15] It would be somewhat unlikely to have this early reference to his passion. A paraphrase probably best suggests the meaning. "Have patience; I will do something after a while."

The statement of Mary to Jesus and her evident expectancy

[15] As far as the Synoptics are concerned, we would not know that the ministry of Jesus was longer than a year. In passing it may be remarked that John's chronology seems more accurate and provides the basis for the generally accepted three-year ministry on the part of scholars. This is one of the factors that make the acceptance of the essential genuineness of John's Gospel not wholly unwarranted.

of some action on his part must have set in motion a train of thought regarding his own place as the Messiah. Jesus had shortly before gone through the period of temptation in the wilderness. Following the high spiritual experience of his baptism he had definitely entered upon his messianic ministry. He now had about him a group of disciples. Can helping in this situation be the will of God?

It was a momentous crisis, and in that hour of perplexity, searching of soul and inquiring after the Father's will, it was revealed to him what "the works of the Messiah" must be—not dazzling marvels, as the Jews expected, but lowly deeds of service and compassion. [16]

Jesus now asked the servants to fill the great stone water pots. They held as much as twenty-five gallons each and were used largely as reservoirs of water for supplying the needs of the household. One interpretation holds that the jars were filled in order to establish the fact that water was being drawn from the well. After the task of filling them had been completed, Jesus said, "Draw out now, and bear unto the governor of the feast." The water that was then drawn was that which was turned into wine. A rather beautiful symbolic interpretation can be given if this view is held. The water that remained water for ceremonial use becomes wine when dedicated to human need. The more generally accepted view is that it was the water in the pots which was turned into wine. He took what he had— the water at hand—and used it to bless men.

Apart from the rustic beauty of this story there are many lessons the author had in mind when he recorded it. One of the most obvious is that blessing resides in anything touched by the hands of our Lord. Water used for washing is turned into such wine of gladness that any feast is graced. It is no ordinary wine. Its quality is such that men marvel at its rare bouquet. So with all of life when Jesus is present and when the richness of his

[16] David Smith, *Days of His Flesh* (8th ed.), p. 57.

personality gives a flavor to living that men shall not forget. Jesus not only provided wine for the feast, but he was abundant in his gifts. The surplus was in the nature of a present to the bride and groom. Our Lord gave liberally and gladly for all human need.

What is the method of the miracle? Is there a rationale that can explain it? The feeble view that there were dregs and sediment of wine in the water pots, which discolored the water and gave it the taste of wine,[17] is so weak and is in such contrast to the exclamation of the master of ceremonies that one should really ignore it. Possibly the best attitude is to ask why be unimaginative enough to try to explain it? In faith let it be accepted in the poetic insight of the statement, "The conscious water saw its God and blushed." The truth here is that Jesus takes what he has and provides an overflowing blessing. His is the full gospel of an abundant life for all men, including brides and bridegrooms in peasant localities. In this day we are beginning to recognize that the message of Jesus is for all phases of life. We can be certain that anything Jesus provided was good and that it was abundant. This is amply established by the jest of the master of ceremonies, "Every man at the beginning doth set forth good wine; and when men have well drunk, then that which is worse: but thou hast kept the good wine until now." This is just what Jesus does. He always keeps the best for those who welcome him to their weddings and into their homes.

Much fruitless discussion has waged around the problem of whether or not the wine was alcoholic. That it contained the small amount of alcohol necessary for preservation is probably true. Let it suffice to remark that it was wine our Master could drink; it was not the product of a commercialized liquor traffic.

---

[17] Ewald, in his *Christus*, p. 328, tried to preserve the religious values by stating that the water tasted like wine because of the enchantment of Christ's spiritual discourse. In his *Leben Jesu*, p. 308, Beyschlag contends that Jesus threw the guests into a hypnotic state. Strauss, in his *Leben Jesu*, II, 218, goes so far as to hint that John was probably intoxicated and shared the delusion of his guests. Simply to record such farfetched interpretations is sufficient answer.

Jesus came to exalt all things his heavenly Father had made—the product of the field, of the vine, of the hand of man. God made all things good. It is man that makes them a curse. Modern Christians need always to remember the words of Jesus, "I am come that they might have life, and that they might have it more abundantly."

It is a healthy indication that the modern church and Christians of today are learning the lesson taught so long ago at a simple wedding in Cana of Galilee—all things are exalted when Jesus touches them. For instance, there was Brayton Case, of the Pyinmana Agricultural School of Burma. Dr. Case often tucked a purebred chicken under one arm and a Poland-China pig under the other and went out to preach to the natives about "Christian chickens and pigs"! Only when chickens, pigs, wheat, gears, motors, airplanes, and every product of man's hand are used for blessing man, rather than cursing him, can we ever hope to have Jesus in our midst or to truly understand the evangelist when he said, "This beginning of miracles did Jesus in Cana of Galilee, and manifested forth his glory."

# 4

## Bread Jesus Blesses

THERE is a universal appeal about a picnic, barbecue, clam-bake, or any other large gathering where folks are eating to-gether, especially in the open where one feels close to both God and nature. From time immemorial eating together has been one of the most natural expressions of social community.

In the gospel records there are a number of different accounts which involve a common sharing of food. The wedding at Cana had its food as well as its wine. Peter's mother-in-law served Jesus and certain other disciples after her own healing. In Sa-maria the disciples went into the village to purchase supplies for the noonday meal. They likewise prepared the food at the Last Supper. Martha busied herself about providing an adequate meal when Jesus came to visit in her home. The women who followed Jesus ministered to the needs of the disciples. This certainly included the preparation of food. Jesus took delight in a quiet dinner in the home where he could have a heart-to-heart talk with Zacchaeus. At a dinner with a certain Pharisee, Jesus watched with interest the seating of the guests. Observing the petty but human play for preferment, Jesus taught power-fully of true humility. More formal banquets, such as the one given him by Simon the Pharisee, were not avoided by Jesus. His enemies with perverted shortsightedness even accused him of being a winebibber and a glutton. Well enough for John the Baptist to subsist on locusts and wild honey; the Son of man came eating and drinking, delighting in the good things his heavenly Father had bestowed so bountifully upon his earthly creatures for their nourishment and enjoyment. In these instances others had prepared the meal for the Master and his followers. In most cases Jesus was the guest.

Apart from the morning by the lakeside when he broiled fish for the disciples, there are two accounts in the gospel records in which Jesus was the host, and the host in the grand manner. One is the incident of the feeding of the four thousand (Mark 8:1-9; Matt. 15:32-39), and the other the feeding of the five thousand. The latter is recorded in the four Gospels: Mark 6: 30-44; Matt. 14:13-21; Luke 9:10-17; John 6:1-13. All scholars feel the admitted difficulties in the accounts. Most critical students hold that the incident involving the four thousand is a duplicate or variant of the other. Yet along with the similarities there are many differences in the two accounts. In the feeding of the four thousand the people have been with Jesus three days. In Mark 8:2 he says, "I have compassion on the multitude, . . . because they have nothing to eat." However, in Mark 6:34, where the account of the feeding of the five thousand is treated, the compassion is because the people "were as sheep not having a shepherd," so Jesus began to teach them. The main point is the stress on the compassion of our Lord. He pitied the "vulgar" multitude both for their physical and for their spiritual wants. Here was a new note. Crowds often are to be feared rather than pitied—especially hungry crowds. Jesus did not see them en masse but as hungry individuals with specific needs. At the heart of the genius of Jesus is this emphasis on the personal. The good shepherd goes out in the storm after the *one* lost sheep. Children hungry for love, and multitudes that needed food were persons to Jesus, not masses of people.

The location for the feeding of the four thousand is probably in Gentile territory in the area of the Greek Decapolis on the east side of the lake. This locale suggests that as Jesus was able to provide for the Jews, he could likewise satisfy the Gentiles. The baskets are of different sizes and uses. Here the hamper is a large one often used for work purposes.

The account of the feeding of the five thousand is located in Bethsaida, probably Bethsaida Julias, on the northern part of the Lake of Galilee just east of the Jordan. The basket mentioned is the small Jewish luncheon basket used to carry food on a journey so the faithful would not have to buy from Gentiles.

The difference in figures is definite. In Mark, Jesus specifically referred to both occasions (8:19-20). A difficulty has correctly been pointed out of understanding how the disciples, after having participated in the feeding of the five thousand, could have asked Jesus in Mark 8:4, "Whence can a man satisfy these men with bread here in the wilderness?" The principal problems in both accounts are the same, so we will pass to the consideration of the story of feeding the five thousand.

Of all the miracles in the Gospels this is the only one recorded by all four evangelists. This is such strong presumptive evidence that something unusual took place that Sholem Asch in his novel *The Nazarene* writes as if it were a genuine miracle. Should the feeding of the four thousand be a variant of this incident, the evidence is that much more weighty for a remarkable feeding. "The story of a feeding was a marked feature of the tradition and very highly valued." [1] The Synoptic Gospels place this feeding after the return of the twelve and the beheading of John the Baptist. This would help to explain the enthusiasm with which the populace received this "sign," and gives a basis for their attempt to make Jesus an earthly ruler. John tells us that it is at the time of the Passover. Mark's reference to "green grass" (6:39) supports this time element, as does the mention of barley loaves, a common food at this season of the year.

It had been an exceedingly busy day. Jesus had responded to many requests for healing. His informal teaching method, involving the answering of specific questions and the giving of generalized truth which grew out of particular life situations,

[1] R. H. Lightfoot, *History and Interpretation in the Gospels*, p. 115.

was most taxing. Yet here were the people, thousands of them, with their normal human needs. He had healed, he had taught, but still the crowd needed so much more that he could give. The Gospels place the incident shortly after the murder of John the Baptist by Herod Antipas. The voice of the magnificent prophet, whom Jesus considered to be outstanding, was stilled. Baptized with John's baptism, Jesus had identified himself intimately with the fearless wilderness prophet. Now he would have to live for John as well as for himself. The multitudes had known John was a prophet, the first in long centuries. John was dead, and with him many a hope had perished. The great heart of Jesus went out to the people who had lost a voice, even as he had lost one whom he greatly admired. The people were truly "as sheep not having a shepherd."

The account has been objected to on numerous grounds: (1) It is a myth which grew out of a similar story of a miraculous feeding by the prophet Elisha (II Kings 4:42-44). It may likewise have been influenced by the Mosaic feeding in the wilderness (Num. 11).

2) It simply could not happen from a rational standpoint. Bernhard Weiss's remarks are pertinent here:

The criticism which is afraid of miracles finds itself in no small difficulty in the presence of this narrative. It is guaranteed by all our sources which rest upon eyewitness; and these show the independence of their tradition by their deviations, which do not affect the kernel of the matter, and cannot be explained by any tendencies whatever. In the presence of this fact the possibility of myth or invention is utterly inadmissible. . . . Only this remains absolutely incontrovertible, that it is the intention of all our reports to narrate a miracle; and by this we must abide, if the origin of the tradition is not to remain an entirely inexplicable riddle. [2]

3) It runs counter to Jesus' policy of refusing to do astounding deeds. In the case of the latter, however, it needs to be

[2] *Leben Jesu*, II, 196-200 (Eng. tr., II, 381-85).

remembered that Jesus considered himself in the line of the prophets. Moses and Elisha had fed the people when they were hungry. It would not be out of keeping for the Son of man to do likewise. Scholars have been right in seeing some parallel. But above all, Jesus never failed to meet human need. He had compassion on the physical as well as the spiritual needs of man. As a realist Jesus knew that people could not be ministered to spiritually if they were hungry physically.

There are two solutions suggested in the record. The first is that of the disciples, "Send them away." The people could have scattered and brought provisions, but it would have been with difficulty. The human need of the hungry multitude would have been removed from the sight of Jesus and the disciples. Sending them away was a natural expedient, but it was not a solution. One tragedy of the twentieth century has been the many deserving appeals for aid. Their very multiplicity is such that one becomes hardened to the cry for help and adopts the expedient of forgetting about the need or putting it out of mind. This may help the conscience, but it does no good in the relief of misery.

The other solution is that propounded by Jesus, "Give ye them to eat" (Mark 6:37). John records that Jesus asked Philip, who was from Bethsaida and hence knew the neighborhood, where they could buy food for the crowd. It is one of those reminiscences which, with Mark's "green grass," suggest an eyewitness account. Jesus saw here a golden opportunity to bind the group together in a new sense of community. The disciples at once point out that their funds are totally insufficient to feed such a vast throng. "Two hundred pennyworth" would not be enough. The modern equivalent might be two hundred or two thousand dollars, depending on the degree of inflation and the caterer engaged! Yet this was not the answer, for Jesus knew what men of faith have always known: God supplies the need for those who have implicit trust in him. Sometimes not immediately, but in the long run, yes.

"Give ye them to eat." Feeding five thousand people with

plenty of provisions is no easy task. It was once my privilege to attend a great barbecue held in connection with a peach festival at Fort Valley, Georgia. The whole countryside was decked in a sunset glow of pink peach blossoms. For miles the dust hung heavy on the roads that led to the little town of Fort Valley. Literally hundreds of pigs, sheep, and steers simmered all day in great pits. About 25,000 people were fed famous Georgia barbecue with a generous helping of Brunswick stew, but it was not accomplished without much and careful planning. Jesus' first command was concerning order. "Have the people sit down by ranks." The soft air of spring, the green of the grass, sparkling Galilee below and God's blue above, gave a setting to grace any banquet. The next move involved what was at hand. A lad offered his lunch, five loaves and two fish. It was such a small supply for such a vast need; no wonder Andrew said, "What are they among so many?" To men of great faith God makes all things possible. The resources may appear small indeed to fill such a large necessity. They are sufficient when divine compassion is linked with God's power. After invoking the blessing of God, Jesus divided the food and began to pass it out to the multitude. He did not turn stones into bread; that would have been magic, not miracle. Jesus took what he had and used that. Barley bread, the food of the poor, was both a coarse bread and one that was used especially in the springtime. Here is another incidental reference which supports the season of the feeding. Five loaves and two fish were sufficient in the hands of Jesus. He always has been able to do mighty things where there is consecration, faith, and trust. Great faith begins to pass out God's bounty at once. The continued exercise of faith is guarantee of sufficiency for all.

Before the bread was broken, it was blessed. The event takes on a sacramental character. Many commentators have considered this the most important of the lessons involved. Observe the sacramental element in Mark 6:41: he *took, looked up, blessed, broke, gave*. It is reminiscent of I Cor. 11:23-34. Yet strangely

enough the account in John, which is followed by a discourse
on the bread of life, is less suggestive of the Last Supper than the
synoptic narratives. After a careful study of the terms in all of
the incidents Alan H. McNeile says decisively:

> In the feedings ... the central act is described in words which re-
> call the Eucharistic act at the Last Supper. ... The conclusion can
> hardly be avoided that in all the meals the evangelists realized that
> there had been a Eucharistic act and expressed it in their wording.
> To the multitudes by the lake, to the Twelve on the night before his
> death and to the disciples at every Eucharistic feast from then till
> now, he gives a foretaste of the Feast in the Messianic Kingdom. [3]

While recognizing the significance of the meal as an anticipation
of the messianic feast, the modern writer who says that the
common meal is of little importance misses the great values the
fellowship of the occasion certainly had.[4] The feeling of community strength was so great the people wanted to make Jesus
their king.

The sacramental nature and the value of a common sharing
of food were indelibly impressed on me in a visit with German
Christians just prior to the sessions of the World Council of
Churches at Amsterdam in the summer of 1948. Food shortages
were still severe in Germany. Our party traveled under a military permit that allowed us to eat in hotels reserved for occu-
pational officials. In them we had adequate food, bordering on the
bountiful. The contrast when we ate as guests of our German
brethren was particularly marked. They gave us their best—
boiled potatoes garnished with the thinnest of gravies, bread
spread with lard, and a cottage cheese dish. That was all, and we
knew that even this had meant real sacrifice for them. To them it
was a banquet prepared for honored guests from across the sea.
But as we partook together, the presence of Christ was strangely
and yet unmistakably with us. The common sharing had brought

[3] *The Gospel According to St. Matthew*, p. 216.
[4] See C. J. Cadoux, *The Historic Mission of Jesus*, p. 243.

a community in Christ we never could have known in lands of plenty.

> The Holy Supper is kept, indeed,
> In whatso we share with another's need.

The simple ritual in which Jesus engaged was one that was quite common among the Jews of his day. They seldom ate without first thanking their heavenly Father for his bounty. Certainly as the throng partook with one another of the food which Jesus had distributed, they were bound together in a fellowship. As the disciples looked back on the incident, it was for them truly a foretaste on a large scale of the establishment of the Lord's Supper. John alone records that the fragments were gathered up at the bidding of Jesus. This fulfilled a customary Jewish provision of saving the leftovers at the end of a meal. The messianic feast was to be bountiful, but along with it all of the proprieties must be observed.

How can these things be? A great crowd simply could not be fed by five loaves and two fish is one answer. Paulus suggested nearly a century ago—and he has been followed by many others —that what actually took place was a sharing of supplies by those who had come prepared with those who had not been so provident. [5] Jesus set the example by dividing the five loaves and two fish, and then the people in the orderly ranks, seeing the generosity of the lad who brought his lunch to Jesus, hauled out their own supplies and shared with those in their group. Those who see in such an explanation a solution find in it even a greater miracle: that of converting a self-regarding mass into an other-regarding group.

The eucharistic parallel has led Albert Schweitzer to believe that Jesus gave an "eschatological sacrament," a minute portion of food, to each one. [6] The eucharistic element is certainly in

[5] *Exegetisches Handbuch*, II, 205-6.
[6] *Quest of the Historical Jesus*, p. 374.

the story, and this was felt particularly in the churches for which the account was first written, yet as a final answer for what took place it does not account for the enthusiastic attempt of the crowd to make Jesus a king.

For those who have no mental reservations in their readiness to accept miracle the answer is that it cannot be rationalized; it is simply a genuine miracle. Our knowledge of natural laws or God's use of them is not sufficient to account for the method that was employed. The Western text (a grouping of important New Testament manuscript sources) makes it clear that Jesus was praying when the loaves were multiplied. We cannot understand how this could have been; but after all, do we not have to accept most of God's gifts without understanding them? How many understand the composition of light before they bask gratefully in the rays of the summer sun? The wise comment of C. S. Lewis is pertinent here.

The two instances of miraculous feeding . . . involve the multiplication of a little bread and a little fish into much bread and much fish. Once in the desert Satan had tempted Him to make bread of stones: He refused the suggestion. "The Son does nothing except what He sees the Father do"; perhaps one may without boldness surmise that the direct change from stone to bread appeared to the Son to be not quite in the hereditary style. Little bread into much bread is quite a different matter. Every year God makes a little corn into much corn: the seed is sown and there is an increase. And men say, according to their several fashions, "It is the laws of Nature," or, "It is Ceres, it is Adonis, it is the Corn-King." But the laws of Nature are only a pattern: nothing will come of them unless they can, so to speak, take over the universe as a going concern. And as for Adonis, no man can tell us where he died or when he rose again. Here, at the feeding of the five thousand, is He whom we have ignorantly worshipped: the *real* Corn-King who will die once and rise once at Jerusalem during the term of office of Pontius Pilate. [7]

Forgetting the question of miracle for a moment, observe on what a human level the whole story places Jesus. There is noth-

[7] *Op. cit.*, p. 164.

ing vague or mystical about him and his services. He is here the host superb, meeting the concrete needs of folks when they are famished. Jesus never let a metaphysical proposition such as whether or not to work a miracle interfere with his alleviation of need. Jesus is a very gracious host who is concerned for the physical well-being of his flock as well as for their spiritual needs. For our own day does not the whole incident teach that Christ's Church should be concerned about social and economic problems, along with its even greater concern about the need of the people for that spiritual bread which is eternal? Even Jesus could not preach to hungry men; he fed them first.

Notice the reactions. The people evidently were persuaded that a miracle had taken place, for they almost immediately tried to make Jesus a king. They wanted to install him as leader of the political revolt against Rome. What a general he would have made! He could have supplied his armies by dividing a few loaves.

Jesus did feed the people to stay their hunger, but John with his deep mystical insight sees the deeper truth and meaning behind the story as he launches immediately into his discourse on the bread of life. The Fourth Gospel tells us that the people followed Jesus to the other side of the lake. There our Lord began a discourse warning against following him simply because of the signs that he wrought. The people had eaten their fill, but they did not catch the deeper significance of what had taken place. Jesus says, "Labor not for the meat which perisheth, but for that meat which endureth unto eternal life." It is the bread of heaven for which we ought to strive. In John's dialogue form the people refer to the Mosaic feeding, "Our fathers did eat manna in the desert." They pictured this experience as a gay picnic—which was certainly not the case to the participants in the march from Egypt to Canaan. The contemporaries of Jesus fell into the error, so common to all of us, of seeing history through rose-colored glasses. "Oh, for the good old days of our fathers when Jehovah rained food from heaven." They overlooked completely the fact these same ancestors had been bitter in their rebellion against the manna. To the spiritually-minded manna is a sign of God's care. It was Jesus who gave true perspective in this matter of food. "The bread of God is he which cometh down from heaven. . . . I am the bread of life." History has surely established that he is. As Matthew Arnold walked on a hot August day through East London's squalid streets, observing the wretchedness of that industrial region, he met by chance a preacher friend. Out of the encounter grew one of his most thought-provoking shorter poems:

> I met a preacher there I knew, and said,—
> "Ill and o'erworked, how fare you in this scene?"
> "Bravely!" said he; "for I of late have been
> Much cheered with thoughts of Christ, *the living bread.*"

One measure of the genius of Jesus is seen in the aptness with which our Lord draws from a local circumstance or incident abiding spiritual truths. As the disciples and their Master passed a flowering Judean hillside, it very likely furnished the locale for such an observation as, "Consider the lilies of the field, how they grow; . . . Solomon in all his glory was not arrayed like one of these. Wherefore, if God clothe [them] . . . , shall he not much more clothe you?"

From such an impressive incident as the feeding of so large a company Jesus would be the first to trust that the disciples and the multitude would learn the spiritual lesson of their common meal together. That such is the case is seen later in Mark (8:14-21), where Jesus rebuked the disciples for their lack of ability to understand what had taken place. The resources of God in Christ are sufficient for the needs of those who will put their trust in him. Jesus fed the multitude in the long ago by Galilee's pleasant waters; so he can feed us today, but we must enter into the equation and eat the bread which he breaks as we make our own his divine type of personality.

"How many loaves have ye?"
Thus spake the Christ by Galilee.

How many loaves have ye?
Jesus thy Saviour still asks of thee,
For the multitudes hunger in deserts drear,
And the cry of their need has reached his ear. [8]

[8] Marian E. Doyle, "Loaves and Fishes."

# 5

## Nature a Servant

I. STILLING THE TEMPEST—*Mark 4:35-41; Matt. 8:18, 23-27; Luke 8:22-25*

ONLY those who have experienced a storm at sea can appreciate the utter sense of helplessness one feels. This is true in a great ocean-going vessel. It is doubly true in a small open boat.

There is a difficulty in placing chronologically the stilling of the tempest. All three of the synoptic accounts vary in the incidents that precede. Matthew and Luke are in all likelihood not chronological in this place in their narratives. Mark, the earliest of the Gospels, places the event near the close of a very busy day for our Lord. Those who punch a clock or keep a weather eye on the forty hours a week man should toil, have difficulty in recognizing how busy a spiritual leader can be. There are some days particularly in which one event after another seems to pile up in a veritable mountain, each incident of which requires an outgoing of vital energy. Even though the chronology here may be in doubt, the fact that Jesus had many such busy days is clear. Mark and Luke agree in placing the account of stilling the tempest just before the healing of the Gerasene demoniac. The importance of this will be seen as we proceed.

According to Mark's chronology Jesus began this day by facing an accusation of being in league with the devil. Imagine, if you can, the kindly, helpful prophet of Nazareth, whose sole passion was to do the will of his heavenly Father by bringing a blessing to his fellow man, facing such a charge. When this

54

accomplished nothing for his accusers, they changed their tac-
tics and asked for a sign. A miracle or two might have morbid
interest even if the wonders were wrought by the help of Satan.
With the scorn due such ungodly inquisitiveness Jesus said that
no sign should be given a wicked and adulterous generation save
that of the prophet Jonah. Almost immediately thereafter Mary
the mother of Jesus, and his brothers sought to take him home to
Nazareth. He had to tell his listeners, as well as the members of
his family, that his mother and brothers were those who were
seeking to do God's will. It is a commentary on the spiritual
resource of Jesus to observe that immediately following these
incidents in which his truth was rejected by those closest to
him the evangelist records some of the most profound teachings
of Jesus about the Kingdom. There follows the great series of
parables—those of the sower, the candlestick, the unconscious
growth, and the grain of mustard. The stilling of the tempest
is closely connected with these parables which precede the
incident.

After such a day it is little wonder that the record tells us that
he entered the boat "even as he was" and fell exhausted with the
toil, his tired head pillowed upon a cushion in the stern of the
vessel. It would scarcely be possible to draw a clearer picture of
the humanity of Jesus. Christians can be ever grateful for the
vividness with which Peter remembered the incident as he recalled Jesus with his head on a pillow. John Mark caught and
preserved the vividness of Peter's preaching. [9] When Jesus entered the boat, he was utterly weary; his body must have rest.
The calm lapping of the waves during the trip across the lake
lulled him into deep and refreshing sleep.

Mark tells us that "other little ships" accompanied the small
vessel that carried Jesus. What a blessed convoy that was! Only
a few could be in the boat with Jesus, but there were other
little ships to carry those who were closest to him. These other

[9] See Manson and Wright, *op. cit.*, p. 73; also my *Peter, the Man Jesus Made*,
pp. 45, 123.

ships shared in the proximity of Jesus, they participated in the danger, but they were also present at the miracle. All could not be in the boat with Jesus, but many could be near him in the other vessels. Venturing with Christ then meant spiritual danger; for too many keepers of the synagogue were ready to shut people out of the Kingdom with their heavy keys. On more than one occasion it also involved physical danger as well.

In all the wide world there is no more interesting small body of water than the Lake of Galilee. It is remarkable in that it lies 680 feet below sea level and yet has sweet and pleasant water. This is made possible by its outlet into the Jordan River, which then tumbles tortuously down to the arid wastes of the Dead Sea, some 1300 feet below sea level. Galilee, whose very name sings of poetry and wondrous words, is about thirteen miles long and eight miles wide. It is shaped much like a pear or a human heart. The hills that rise abruptly on either side are divided by gullies down which winds often howl to the surface of the lake. Violent squalls are a commonplace. On this particular day the storm was of sufficient strength to alarm even experienced fishermen and boatmen.

One who had not thought too deeply on such matters might ask, Why did God permit such a storm to endanger the lives of his Son and all the holy apostles? Was not the whole future Christian faith put in jeopardy by the caprice of a summer wind and the pounding of lake waves? Such a critic forgets that Jesus taught that his heavenly Father would play no favorites for the righteous. In the new Kingdom of God, as in the old theocracy of Jehovah, there were to be no privileges of nature for the Christian. "For he maketh his sun to rise on the evil and on the good, and sendeth rain on the just and on the unjust." (Matt. 5:45.) Wise man that he was, Jesus saw that were such privileges granted, a cheap premium would be placed upon godliness. Following God's way would then become the method of receiving special favors. The God who inhabits the reaches of eternity and who hung out Orion and the Pleiades would be transformed from the Holy One of old into the indulgent keeper of a celestial commissary whose rewards were passed out to those who had happened to join the right political, or shall we say religious, party. Jesus understood that God's children could not be spared adversity. Later Paul writes of him, "He . . . spared not his own Son, but delivered him up for us all" (Rom. 8:32). In his own life he learned obedience by the things which he suffered. His disciples, even though they are to us the holy apostles, are not greater than their Lord. His followers must learn to turn their tragedies into triumphs. Jesus himself has set the example in the great alchemy of adversity which can turn the lead of frail humanity into the gold of strong Christian character—but not without trial!

As the storm raged, the experienced boatman, Peter, struggled with the sails, ordered the boom to be lashed, wrestled with the tiller, even as he shouted orders to the others to bail. Despite all their efforts the storm continued to howl with unabated fury until finally Peter, despairing of their lives and of the life of his teacher asleep through all the turmoil, awakened Jesus somewhat rudely and shouted, "Carest thou not that we perish?" Both Matthew and Luke shun this expression. It must have been Peter. He was ever the spokesman for the disciples and was brash enough on more than one occasion to speak words of reproach to Jesus. Peter had cause to be both frightened and alarmed. As a seaman he knew how serious was the circumstance. The boat was in all likelihood overloaded. The cry for help was instinctive rather than reasoned. It was a plea asking Jesus, the leader, to take command. True, he was a carpenter, not a sailor, but he possessed qualities of leadership that made men turn to him. The disciples did not necessarily expect a miracle. They simply looked to Jesus for the help and leadership they felt he could give.

Jesus, awaking from a sound sleep, surveyed the situation with a glance. The terror of the moment, the peril of the boatmen, the lashing fury of the waves, were all a part of the picture. All three accounts have him rebuking both the wind and the waves. Jesus uses a curious phrase, "Be muzzled." It was the same word employed in Mark 1:25 to silence the demon. This has occasioned the suggestion that Jesus was speaking to the excited one who awakened him rather than to the storm itself. However, storms were commonly thought of as the work of demons. McNeile says that the whole incident is related, not because of the miracle, but as an evidence of the subduing of all evil powers, which was a definite sign of the nearness of the Kingdom. [10] This is supported by the account of healing the Gerasene demoniac which immediately follows. The Oriental often personalized the forces of nature. In the psalms we find evidence of this, "Stormy wind fulfilling his word" (148:8). Jesus here is addressing an apostrophe to the storm. It was more than an apostrophe; it was a prayer of supreme trust. To the quaking disciples he asks, "Where is your faith?" Dramatic as it was, the whole incident is in character. Here is the same one speaking who saw God's will in the rain falling upon the evil as well as the good. If God's good world is beset by a storm, then still it. Here was "a spontaneous expression of victorious faith and heroic self-possession." [11]

The record goes on, "And there was a great calm." The wind ceased, the waves died down, and the storm was stilled. "What manner of man is this, that even the wind and the sea obey him?" What more natural termination could we have to the story whose vividness, suspense, and naturalness are unsurpassed in the Gospels? It "contributes a brief but vivid picture of the journeyings in and around Galilee, and of the impression which Jesus made upon His followers." [12]

There are several positions in addition to the one considered above that have been held: It was a coincidence that the storm

[10] *Op. cit.,* p. 111.

[11] A. B. Bruce, *The Miraculous Element in the Gospels,* p. 211.

[12] B. H. Branscomb, *The Gospel of Mark* ("Moffatt New Testament Commentary"), p. 88.

subsided very shortly after the naïve apostrophe of Jesus. The conjuncture of the two events made a profound impression on the disciples. This satisfies those who have preconceived views of the impossibility of miracle and yet who know the record well enough to appreciate that something extraordinary took place.

Another view is that Jesus simply observed that the storm was about to end anyway. If this is the case, the statement is thoroughly out of keeping with what we know of Jesus. The words "Be muzzled," translated "Peace, be still," were as genuine as any Jesus ever uttered, and were wrung from him in the excitement and in the faith of the moment. He was a good observer of nature, but he had no time to cast a weather eye to the heavens and see the possibilities of the storm's subsidence. The one who said, "A wicked and adulterous generation seeketh after a sign; and there shall be no sign given unto it," would not have used a keen weather discernment to foist a belief in powers he did not possess.

The third view is that the tempest did cease and that the calm was somehow connected with the apostrophe of Jesus, which was both a command and a prayer. Such a view is not inconsistent with the general position that God plays no favorites by granting privileges of nature to those who serve him. The man of faith and the man of prayer find no difficulty. [13] In the ordinary course of events God grants no special favors for believers, yet *the resources of heaven are on tap when moral and spiritual ends will be served by answered prayer.*

There are well-authenticated instances in Christian history that make the doubting of such a statement a true miracle of unbelief. One incident I myself witnessed. It was in the summer of 1926. The evangelistic committee of the Calvary Baptist Church, New York City, was conducting a special tent program in a new area in Queens, L.I. The fourteen-year-old girl evange-

[13] See George A. Buttrick's magnificent discussion of this whole problem in his *Prayer*, Chapters 6 and 7.

list, Uldine Utley, was preaching. All during her message the rain poured down in torrents, keeping up such a drumbeat upon the tent that one heard with difficulty. At the close of the sermon Miss Utley prayed with the simple trust of a child and asked God for the rain to cease so that the plea to accept the way of Christ might be made with no disturbance. It was a brash and daring thing that those of us with less faith would not have presumed to do, but I was there, and the rain stopped immediately. Coincidence? Well, yes, that is one explanation, but only one.

Jesus made no effort to prove that he was lord of nature when he uttered those arresting words, "Peace, be still," in the stern of that little vessel. He did have faith to believe that nature existed, not for itself, but ultimately for moral ends; consequently he showed no fear in the face of storm. Franklin D. Elmer, Jr., has caught this truth:

> Who struggles up the tortuous peaks
> Roams the hills with easy stride.
> Who storms across the widest seas
> Embarks upon a pond with casual mien.
> Who beholds the majesty of God
> Is fearless in the presence of mortality. [14]

We might say that Jesus was here giving a dramatic laboratory demonstration of the truth which this blasé age of ours has yet to learn. It was William Temple who wrote:

The uniformity of nature is grounded in the purpose of God. But when that purpose would be itself defeated by some anticipated occurrence, that occurrence is in fact impossible—as Christ suggested when he met the alarm of his disciples with the implication that the boat which carried the hope of the world could not sink. The astonishment of the disciples is that the storm ceased at his bidding—a minor matter. His astonishment was that they had any anxiety.[15]

Turning to the disciples Jesus asks, "Have you no faith?"

[14] "Confidence." *Christian Century*, Aug. 4, 1948. Used by permission.
[15] *Nature, Man and God*, p. 268.

One is tempted to paraphrase and expand on what must have been in the mind of our Lord. "Do you not know that God's purposes even in a tempest are good? No storm, no matter what its results, can bring ultimate harm to those who are serving God." Jesus knew there was danger, jeopardy, and uncertainty in the storm, and that it was all genuine. Jesus does not question the concern of the disciples—that was a normal, human reaction. He does question their lack of faith in the concern. Kierkegaard saw truly when he wrote, "Without risk there is no faith. Faith is precisely the contradiction between the infinite passion of the individual's inwardness and the objective uncertainty." [16] E. Stanley Jones has put it, "Faith is not believing in spite of evidence; it is acting in disregard of consequences."

There is and always has been peace where Jesus is. Today he brings peace of soul; is it too much to expect that tomorrow he will bring that external peace among the sons of men? Angels first sang of it on that far Judean night when shivering shepherds warmed their hearts with the music and the prophecy, "Glory to God in the highest, and on earth peace, good will toward men," as they told of the birth of a baby whose name was to be "Jesus, for he would save his people from their sins."

Peace within and without! Do you recall a favorite number for certain choirs a generation ago? There is real Christian understanding in it.

*Query:*    Master, the tempest is raging!
            The billows are tossing high!
            The sky is o'ershadowed with blackness,
            No shelter or help is nigh;

            "Carest Thou not that we perish?"—
            How canst Thou lie asleep,
            When each moment so madly is threat'ning
            A grave in the angry deep?

[16] Robert Bretall, ed., *Concluding Unscientific Postscript, a Kierkegaard Anthology*, p. 215.

*Answer*: "The winds and the waves shall obey My will,
Peace, be still! Peace, be still!
Whether the wrath of the storm-tossed sea,
Or demons, or men, or whatever it be,
No water can swallow the ship where lies
The Master of ocean and earth and skies;
They all shall sweetly obey My will;
Peace, be still!
They all shall sweetly obey My will;
Peace, peace, be still!"

## II. CURSING OF THE FIG TREE—*Mark 11:12-14, 20-24; Matt. 21:18-22*

Jesus was not awed by nature; neither was he sentimental about it. Whatever one may think about the incident in connection with the fig tree, the account underscores this fact. It has caused no end of discussion among Bible scholars as well as certain modern moralists. The considerable difficulties in the accounts have occasioned much ingenuity on the part of apologists.

Three incidents connected with a fig tree should be kept in mind. The first is Luke's parable found in Luke 13:6-9. Here is a clear reference to the unfruitfulness of Israel. Consequently Israel will be cut off. Some scholars find this the source for the account of the withering of the fig tree in Mark and Matthew. The over-all application is the same, although there is a difference in the detail of cutting down a tree in one case and withering the tree to prevent future fruit growing in the other. Even such an extremely conservative writer as David Smith calls the latter "an acted parable." [17] Joseph Klausner feels that the story was transformed by the disciples into "a strange miracle inflicting a gross injustice on a tree which was guilty of no wrong and had but performed its natural function." [18]

The difficulty for moralists comes in the fact that Mark says

[17] *Op. cit.*, p. 395.
[18] *Jesus of Nazareth*, p. 269.

it was the Passover season, but goes on to record, "The time of figs was not yet." There might have been something on the tree which could have been eaten, possibly even figs left from the previous year. This seems to be a well-attested possibility. In the vicinity of Jerusalem the Passover season was early for figs, but as long as the leaves were out on a tree, fruit could be expected.

Mark's statement that it was not the time for figs, along with the blasting of a perfectly good tree, shocks present-day moral sensibilities. This would not be the case in the time of Jesus. Subjective and modern viewpoints are no indication of the actual situation in the first century. Even so great a scholar as Adolf Deissmann erred here. He tells of having a fig tree planted in a tub at this home in Berlin. When referring in class to this incident, he usually was able to take a green leaf in February to show his students. One severe winter, however, the tree was killed. His own subjective reaction is clearly seen when he contends that Jesus would not have used the tree in this fashion because "to destroy a tree *appears to me* to be actually sinful." [19] A good deal of sentimentalism has gathered around thinking about our Lord that has little benefit of the actual conditions of his day. Jesus was not a romanticist in his view of nature, such as Rousseau, Wordsworth, or Thoreau. He had an unusual appreciation for God's world, the birds in it, the flowers of the field, and the steadiness of growth; but this was not a subject for idealization on the part of Jesus. He saw and believed in the world about him, but he never went into rhapsodies over a sunset. He said that even Solomon was not clothed as gorgeously as a lily, but his point was that God cares for men. Jesus rejoiced in the bounty provided for the needs of men as the earth brought forth abundantly, but his was a realistic rather than a romantic view. It was God's world, and to be recognized as such. God had made all parts of it. They were all subject to his will. Flowers, fig trees, or birds were a happy illustration of God's

[19] *The Religion of Jesus and the Faith of Paul,* pp. 98 ff. Italics mine.

bounty, but they were subject to his will; and if any one or all of them could provide a lesson for men, who were of much greater value than many sparrows, Jesus did not hesitate to employ them in such a fashion. A good deal of false sympathy has been bestowed upon the Gerasene swine, as well as upon the fig tree. Such views would have been strange to Jesus, for he did not think in these terms.

C. S. Lewis calls the withering of the fig tree "Christ's single miracle of Destruction." [20] The story as we have it is one of judgment which does drive home with powerful intensity the nature and conditions of a fruitful life. The whole incident furnishes a healthy corrective to a modern sentimental view of a "gentle" Jesus. On more than one occasion Jesus showed a divine indignation which adds to his character rather than detracts from it.

Both this account and the preceding one of stilling the storm show that nature was to be used by men. To Jesus the natural world was his Father's world. Its bounty was for men, and whatever lessons it could occasion were likewise for men.

> This is my Father's world,
> O let me ne'er forget
> That though the wrong seems oft so strong,
> God is the Ruler yet. [21]

[20] *Op. cit.*, p. 168.
[21] By Maltbie D. Babcock. Used by permission Charles Scribner's Sons, publisher.

# 6

## It Happened on Galilee

THERE has always been a romance about lakes. What visions of literature, poetry, and our own experience are conjured up in our minds by the mention of Loch Lomond, of Geneva, or turquoise-blue Leman, to say nothing of our American lakes, Champlain, Seneca, Erie, and Tahoe. But of all earth's lakes there is far more romance about Galilee than any of the rest. It was on and about the pleasant waters of this lake that Jesus taught. He knew the beauties of its pear shape, set like a jewel in the Galilean hills. Its dimensions, thirteen miles long by eight wide, made it far more than a pond, even though it is not the largest of lakes. After the heat and toil of the day Jesus often experienced refreshment and rest for his weary body and mind by the cool, limpid waters of Galilee.

> Although my eyes may never see
> That hallowed Lake of Galilee,
>
> Still I have found each little lake
> More fraught with meaning for His sake. [1]

Apart from the account of the stilling of the tempest, which is considered separately, there are three miracles intimately associated with Jesus and the Lake of Galilee. In connection with these stories, as with all of the records of the mighty deeds of Jesus, our first concern should be with what the accounts are

[1] "My Galilees" from *The Blue Platter*, copyright 1945 by Belle Chapman Morrill. Used by permission.

endeavoring to say rather than with a rationale for what took place.

## I. The Draught of Fish—*Luke 5:1-11; John 21:1-14*

From the beginning of time men have been fascinated and intrigued by fish stories. Man is an inveterate fisherman. As he has become more civilized, he has added a wealth of paraphernalia to his fishing equipment, but not by one jot has his interest in fishing abated. The fantastic character of fish stories is almost a byword. In this day of photographs the record of a huge fish or a huge catch can be preserved for others to gaze upon with wonder, even though one has heard stories of photographs that have been retouched! Izaak Walton long ago said, "Fishing deserves commendations. It is an art worthy the knowledge and practice of a wise man."

In both Luke and John we find a record of a miraculous draught of fish. Luke's account places the incident very early in the ministry of Jesus, at the time of the call of Peter to discipleship. The silence of Mark regarding a draught of fish at the time of the call of the disciples makes a problem. Harnack's view [2] that the story was originally derived from the lost ending of Mark may furnish the answer. The possibility of genuine supplemental material cannot be overlooked. It is possible that the draught of fish preceded the call of Peter and was likely influential in his decision, though not actually united with it. Mark therefore omitted the incident; whereas Luke, with his love for the picturesque and dramatic, brings the two incidents together.

The accounts in Luke and John so closely parallel each other that there is certainly some relation between them. Tradition in the Early Church seems clear concerning a wonderful catch of fish by the disciples on Galilee which took place in connection with the presence of the Lord. Bernard feels that both accounts are derived from a Galilean tradition about Christ's ap-

---

[2] *Luke the Physician* (Eng. tr.), p. 227.

pearance to Peter after his resurrection and the restoration of
Peter to the office of an apostle. [3] The reference in Luke 5:8
"Depart from me; for I am a sinful man," would be particularly
appropriate after the resurrection.

Although the Johannine version suggests a highly allegorical
interpretation in some ways, it gives a more natural setting.
"The disciples are at sea, after a long night's fruitless labor,
when the stranger on the shore bids them drop the net on the
right side of the boat; they do not, like Peter in Luke, deliberately put out to sea to catch the miraculous draught." [4] John
definitely places the incident among the resurrection appearances of Jesus. When we understand how the Gospels came to
be written, we recognize that here may be an instance of a so-
called "doublet" account, in which the same incident is pictured
under slightly different circumstances. Peter's statement about
his sinfulness is more meaningful in connection with his denial
of Jesus just prior to the crucifixion and the resurrection experience which followed. At the same time Jesus' call to Peter to be
"a fisher of men" would more naturally be associated with the
beginning of the ministry of Jesus. It is possible that a second
draught of fish and the disciples' reaction to it would have more
meaning if there had been a similar incident some years before.
There is some indication of this in the beloved disciple's simple
and almost naïve statement, "It is the Lord."

Going back to Luke's account: Jesus of Nazareth had gained
a remarkable reputation as a teacher in and about the lovely and
fertile land of Galilee. A carpenter by trade, Jesus was a teacher
by divine call. Remarkable crowds had followed upon his early
ministry. Every man in Galilee knew about the rabbi from Nazareth. Peter and his companions were even more aware of this
new prophet, for it is very likely that they had accompanied
Jesus for a time when he first began to preach. Jesus now began
a ministry which he had every confidence would be significant

[3] *Op. cit.*, p. 689.
[4] J. M. Creed, ed., *The Gospel According to St. Luke*, p. 73.

and permanent. As John had disciples, so must he have his disciples. [5] Who would make more faithful followers than those rough fishermen who had been earnest enough to follow first the prophet John?

The multitude was pressing upon Jesus as it always did in the early days of his ministry. This crowding was so insistent that Jesus felt he must have relief from jostling in order to address effectively the rest. On the lake above were two fishing boats. In one Simon Peter was finishing the weary task of putting things shipshape after a disappointing night's toil. The request of Jesus to push out a little from the land was a welcomed break of routine. The boat furnished a rude but practical place of vantage for the teacher of Nazareth. When he had finished speaking, Jesus turned to Simon and said, "Launch out into the deep, and let down your nets for a draught." The carpenter was telling the fisherman how to run his business. Peter listened avidly to the words of Jesus, but this invasion of his own domain was just a little too much. Simon replied, "Master, we have toiled all the night, and have taken nothing: nevertheless at thy word I will let down the net." He likely thought, "We are tired; we have cleaned our gear and stowed it away, and now you tell us to start out in the daytime, when fish are caught at night. You are asking us to go into deep water. All of our lives have been lived on this lake, and we have always caught fish in shallow water."

Evidently with some reluctance and much doubt Peter took the suggestion of Jesus and lowered the net. To his amazement he pulled it up loaded with great fish. Peter's next words, "Depart from me; for I am a sinful man, O Lord," are typical of his impulsiveness and in full keeping with the circumstances. They were a vivid recognition of the vast difference between the Carpenter and the fisherman. Peter had gained a higher idea of Jesus and a lower one of himself. Both of these attitudes are quite essential to true discipleship.

[5] See John Wick Bowman's discussion in his *Intention of Jesus*, pp. 209-19.

Peter, James, and John were no strangers to Jesus, nor he to them. Disciples of John the Baptist, they had heard his prophetic voice, "He that cometh after me is mightier than I." Could this mighty one be Jesus of Nazareth? They had followed him for a while some time previously. With every indication of a continuing significant ministry, Jesus knew he needed a group of men upon whom he could depend. What finer material could there be than these sturdy, honest fishermen so representative of the best in Israel? So Jesus said, "Come after me, and I will make you fishers of men." They could understand that language. Jesus may have been a carpenter, but he was not a bad amateur as a fisherman! He knew less than Peter about how to fish, but he knew where the fish were, and that makes all the difference in the world. His was a language of the common people, and he spoke it with a persuasiveness that still wins disciples to him.

Beside the impact made upon these three men who were to prove of such importance, what does the incident mean? With Jesus there can be no failure. Jesus is interested in winning masses of men. The disciples are to be fishers, not mere anglers. The net is to be cast out for large hauls. They must work together. The disciples of Jesus have to haul the net in, not singly but with united strength. The haul was far larger than they had any right to expect. God always gives blessings in an overflowing degree. A fulfillment of this challenge and prophecy of Jesus, Peter saw on the day of Pentecost when three thousand were won to Christ.

John's account comes as an appendix to the Gospel. [6] Here it is very evidently an incident in connection with the resurrection appearance of Jesus. If there is a common story behind both Luke and John, there is some evidence that makes this appearance the first manifestation of the Risen Christ to Peter. This is seen in the second-century gospel of Peter, which apparently

---

[6] The problem presented by a possible doublet is recognized; however, the incidents are treated separately because of the complete difference in background as well as the difference in teaching.

leads up to some such appearance as this. The twofold motive behind the account in John is, first, to identify the anonymous disciple as John, son of Zebedee, thus securing apostolic authority for the Gospel; and, second, to restore Peter to his place of authority. Peter and the disciples have left the environs of Jerusalem. The tragedy of the crucifixion has been lost in the wonder of the resurrection. What is more natural than that Peter with the others would wish to go back for a season to the country of their birth, to the lake which had given them a living and from whose borders they had been called to follow Jesus and to become fishers of men? After such climactic experiences to get back into the familiar fishing boat and upon the quieting waters would be good for all of them. Peter announced, "I go a fishing." Thomas, Nathanael, James, and John, with two unnamed disciples, accompanied Peter. Toiling through the night they had caught nothing. The disappointment that all fishermen know was theirs. Toward morning they saw a figure on the shore who inquired concerning their catch. They replied that they had taken nothing. A shout came back, "Cast the net on the right side of the ship, and ye shall find." They did so, and soon the net was loaded with 153 large fish. If Luke's account is correctly placed and there are two separate incidents, the beloved disciple remembered the incident of some time before. Quietly he said to Peter, "It is the Lord." After the disciples had followed the instructions of the Stranger and had experienced a great haul, there was no question about who the Figure was. Peter may not have been the first to recognize Jesus, but he wanted to be the first to get to him, so he jumped overboard and half-swam and half-waded ashore. This action is in complete character with what we know of Peter. So Peter, who had denied so vigorously, is restored completely. As there was not only forgiveness for Peter but also restoration to position and authority, so there is not only forgiveness but also restoration for all who have sinned and fallen short of the glory of God. The only prerequisite is penitence. "And be ye kind one to another, tenderhearted, *for-*

*giving one another, even as God for Christ's sake hath forgiven you.*" (Eph. 4:32.)

From the earliest days of biblical commentaries the number 153 has been considered symbolic. All kinds of fanciful ideas to explain the number have been broached. The suggestion of Jerome [7] is the most likely: The 153 fish refer to the 153 known species of fish according to Latin and Greek historians. In other words, the disciples of Jesus who were to be fishers of men must proclaim an inclusive and universal gospel. The gospel writer is saying that the Church is the vessel ultimately to hold all races of men. Its mission is to all, and success will come when the disciples are obedient to the commands of its divine head. At the close of the first century the Church knew her mission was world-wide, but it is not until our own day that we have seen the gospel ship literally enclose representatives from all races and classes and nations. We are not going to be any more content than were first-century Christians until all men, of all 153 varieties, are ensnared in the meshes of God's love as revealed in Christ Jesus our Lord. Well did Amsterdam say:

As we have studied evangelism in its ecumenical setting we have been burdened by a sense of urgency. We have recaptured something of the spirit of the apostolic age, when the believers "went everywhere preaching the word." If the Gospel really is a matter of life and death, it seems intolerable that any human being now in the world should live out his life without ever having the chance to hear and receive it. [8]

Forgetting the matter of allegory and symbolism, let us take the account at its face value. Here is one of the resurrection appearances of Jesus. He had promised to meet his disciples in Galilee (Matt. 26:32); here he was, and he was alive! How better to prove the reality of the appearance than to relive a former vivid experience in his ministry with the disciples. How better

[7] See Major, Manson, and Wright, *op. cit.*, p. 949.
[8] *The Church's Witness to God's Design*, Report of Section II.

to know that he was not a phantom than to count and recount the 153 fish until they remembered the exact number and passed it carefully on?

## II. WALKING ON THE LAKE—*Matt. 14:22-33; Mark 6:45-52; John 6:15-21*

This incident follows immediately in point of time the feeding of the five thousand and the revolutionary plot to proclaim Jesus a political Messiah. It is best understood in the light of the happenings of that day.

There had been much excitement in connection with the feeding of the multitude. When one understands the electric expectancy with which the whole populace of Palestine was looking for a political deliverer, whom they thought of as the Messiah or Anointed of God, the remarkable works of Jesus would normally cause the people to think, "This is the man." The gospel record is witness to the fact that the whole concept of a political leader was completely repugnant to Jesus. He came to give men God's truth, to win men's souls. His was a spiritual kingdom, and the spiritual nature of it had to be kept uppermost in the minds of his immediate followers. Jesus recoiled from every attempt to make him the political deliverer of the people's dreams. In reacting from the inner struggle to maintain the high concepts of his mission Jesus needed to go constantly to his heavenly Father in prayer. So the disciples were sent across the lake by boat, and Jesus climbed a near-by hill to pray.

Many a message has been preached on the strength that comes from high solitude. Jesus knew and sought its energizing factors. "It is through the intuitions of silence—the deep soul-convictions which escape words and cannot brook the atmosphere of the crowd and its chatter—that we reach God." [9] William Penn, a mystic who had learned much from his Master, in a choice little volume, *Fruits of Solitude*, wrote:

[9] C. G. Lang, *The Miracles of Jesus* (12th ed.), p. 171.

Till we are persuaded to stop and step aside out of the noisy Crowd and incumbering Hurry of the world, and calmly take a prospect of things, it will be impossible we should be able to make a right adjustment of ourselves. That is it—to step aside and take a prospect of things. The wise man is he who from time to time withdraws from the crowd and looks at it from the standpoint of the eternal, and then enters it as one who has discovered his own true path and place in it.

Mark tells us that the disciples were sent to Bethsaida. Matthew follows Mark's lead here, mentioning that they landed in the region of Gennesaret. John tells us that they were going to Capernaum. Harmonists have followed John and have suggested Gennesaret as the final mooring place after stopping at Capernaum. The wind blowing down the wadi Haman was against the disciples, so they toiled "in rowing; for the wind was contrary." Jesus from his vantage point on the hillside during the fourth watch of the night, between three and six A.M., saw the black dots that were the boats of his disciples tossed by the storm. He had promised that he would come to them. The record tells us that he noticed their distress and "cometh unto them, walking upon the sea." Mark adds a peculiar note, "[He] would have passed by them." This provides a difficulty which heightens the historical accuracy of the whole record, as does Mark's conclusion to the story, "They considered not the miracle of the loaves: for their heart was hardened." Seeing the figure, *all* of the disciples cried out, thinking it to be an apparition. It was not the delusion of one excited man. Jesus called, "Take heart, it is I; have no fear" (R.S.V.). Who cares for men who are storm-tossed? Jesus does! There is an affirmation with a ring in it and a great story back of it. In the darkest night, when the trial is great and hope is confused, he comes, walking on the waves if necessary.

Matthew adds the interesting account of Peter's coming to Jesus on the water. This item, with Peter's impulsiveness followed by his doubts, is typical of him; there is a burst of faith

73

succeeded by his self-questioning of his own motives. A problem to the serious student is why did not Mark mention this incident if Mark is based on the reminiscences of Peter? [10] There is no adequate answer. At best we know all too little of what took place in the development of the gospel records. Mark could have missed that particular sermon in which Peter referred to this incident. Or Peter may have refrained from mentioning it because of his intimate relation to the event and the questions that would naturally arise regarding his own participation in the miracle. There are a number of instances involving Peter that Matthew alone records. He evidently had source material that the other evangelists did not possess.

The whole incident has been occasion for much unbelief and satire. The rationalist of the eighteenth and nineteenth centuries endeavored to explain it away—Jesus was really walking on the shore or on a sand bar just under the surface of the water. There are generally admitted difficulties in connection with the incident, two of which are noticed above. John uses the words "straightway"—not one of his favorites—"the boat was at the land" (A.S.V.). This is an indication that they were nearer the shore than they realized. In fact, if we had John's account alone, there is no evidence of miracle. Incidentally, this shows that John is not as fond of the miraculous as some would believe. Rudolph Otto, in discussing this miracle at length,[11] holds that John contains the story in its simplest form, Mark makes it more of a wonder, and finally Matthew gives the complete heightening with its incident of Peter's attempt to come to Jesus on the water. This, of course, is a complete reversal of the generally accepted gospel development. However, the fair student must admit that the difficulties in Mark show that the story in its original forms presented problems. The Greek word *epi* can mean "by" as well as "upon," but all of our versions are correct in translating it "upon." There may well have been an

---

[10] This is the generally accepted position of New Testament scholarship.
[11] *The Kingdom of God and the Son of Man*, pp. 368-69.

unusual set of circumstances to which the record only partially witnesses, yet it is also wise to remember that there are more things in heaven and earth than are dreamt of in our philosophy.

In connection with this event one need not believe that a natural law was violated. No adequate rationale for miracle has ever held to a capricious universe in which "natural" laws are bandied about. To accept miracle the position one must hold is that God knows more about "natural" law than man does, and is willing to utilize his knowledge on occasion. Walking on the water seems incredible, but walking on frozen water is not at all impossible, as we have all witnessed. There is an interesting story that comes out of pioneer Christian work in Africa. A missionary tried to explain this account to an African chief by telling him that in his own country at certain seasons of the year he himself had walked across the river near his home. According to the story not only did the chief put the missionary down as a liar, but it was with difficulty that he escaped with his life. I once used a simple demonstration in my own pulpit when preaching on this incident. Take an ordinary needle which has been held in the fingers until it has accumulated some of the body oils, drop it carefully on the water in a glass, and it will float. The solid steel bar, much heavier than the water it displaces, does not sink because another natural law, that of cohesion, has entered into the equation.

Certain students have seen in this incident a reading of the Christ of faith back into the Jesus of history. If so, it is a remarkable testimony to the Jesus of history. Jesus did not come to his weary disciples as a political deliverer, nor do we have to believe that he came as a phantom messiah whose body was free from the law of gravity, but come he did where there was need. Of John's Gospel, where no miracle is involved, Otto remarks, "Unintentionally the passage plainly testifies to an 'appearance' comforting and helping in great need." [12] There may be a parallel in the

[12] *Op. cit.,* p. 370.

account of the transfiguration. It is one of those remarkable spiritual experiences which simply cannot be explained.

Whenever disciples were storm-tossed then, Jesus came to them; whenever we are anguish-tossed today, Jesus comes to us. In the remarkable account that John Whittaker has given us of the days he and the other companions of Eddie Rickenbacker spent on a rubber raft in the South Pacific during World War II, all of the men testified to the consciousness of a Presence with them on the raft. When they desperately needed rain, they saw a squall in the distance, but the wind was blowing the clouds away.

Whittaker prayed: "It is in your power, God, to send back that rain. It's nothing to You, but it means life to us. God, the wind is yours. You own it. Order it to blow back that rain to us who need it." There are some things that can't be explained by natural law. The wind did not change, but the receding curtain of rain stopped where it was. Then, ever so slowly, it began moving back toward us—against the wind! Maybe a meteorologist can explain that to your satisfaction. One tried it with me; something about a crosscurrent buffeting the squall back. I tell you there was no buffeting. It moved back with a majestic deliberation. It was as though a great omnipotent hand moved it back across the waves. And for my money that's exactly what happened. [13]

Matthew says, "They that were in the ship came and worshipped him, saying, Of a truth thou art the Son of God" (14: 33). He is here using a messianic rather than a theological term. Its full theological implications are a later development. There is dawning messianic recognition which later came to its full flower in the great confession at Caesarea-Philippi. Montefiore feels that this scene deprives that at Caesarea-Philippi of its special importance. [14] However, does it not rather give a psychological background that fits in perfectly with the corporate recognition

[13] As printed in the *Detroit Free Press*, Jan. 18, 1943, under the title, "We Thought We Heard the Angels Sing."

[14] *Synoptic Gospels*, II, 220.

of messiahship at Caesarea-Philippi, where Peter was the spokesman for the disciples? The purpose of both Matthew and Mark
involved a delineation of superhuman powers on the part of our
Lord. Job's reference to the Creator, "[He] treadeth upon the
high places of the sea" (9:8 A.S.V.) could likely have influenced
both evangelists.

## III. THE COIN IN THE MOUTH OF THE FISH—*Matt. 17:24-27*

This is the incident of the temple tax of half a shekel which
every adult male Jew was required to pay for the maintenance
of the temple worship (Exod. 30:11-13). It was not a Roman
tax. From the standpoint of the state religion there was no reason
why Jesus and his disciples were exempt from this obligation.
The account is evidence of an effort on the part of the colloquial
temple authorities to put Jesus and his followers "on the spot."
Their reaction to this demand would disclose to the Jerusalem
ecclesiastical leaders whether the movement connected with the
rabbi of Nazareth involved a revolt against the temple.

The incident is another of those Petrine stories found only in
Matthew. The setting is Capernaum. Jesus had evidently resided
for sufficient time with Peter to be subject to the tax. When
Peter was asked whether his master would pay, he faltered out
a "Yes" and then hurried to Jesus because there was nothing
with which to pay. Jesus replied by telling Peter to pay the tax
for both of them with the coin he would find in a fish. The ring
of Polycrates is a familiar example of stories connected with
wealth found in fish. There are two observations about the account: First, there is no actual record of a miracle. Peter may or
may not have found such a coin. Second, if there is a miracle,
it would be out of character with the Matthew temptation
record of Jesus' refusing to use his power for his own benefit.
The account as we have it does not demand a miracle. It was
perfectly in keeping for Jesus as an Oriental to use this picturesque method of telling Peter to go catch a fish and pay the
tax with the proceeds. For those who wish to believe that an

unusual event occurred there is nothing improbable in a fish's swallowing a bright object or in its being recovered. If this is the case, the miracle involves foreknowledge on the part of Jesus.

In the ancient East victorious or ruling classes were exempt from taxation; they were the kings' "sons." With an interesting twist of language Jesus here uses this fact to make a clear claim for a unique relationship to the temple and the God of the temple. The Son does not have to pay the tax; he is free. Yet in the account Jesus recognizes his obligation to organized religion, "Lest we cause them to stumble, go and pay the tax." Later in the history of the Church this story evidently served well the Jewish Christians who were concerned as to their correct relation to the temple tax.

Galilee will forever be connected in the hearts and the minds of the faithful throughout the earth with the glorious ministry of our Lord. Whatever one believes about the miraculous draught, the coin found in the mouth of the fish, or the record of walking upon the water, the primary factor for modern disciples is that Jesus, who walked by its sweet waters, still walks with us today.

> I tramped the pavements, cursing God,
> When there beside me Jesus trod!
>
> Now we shall walk, my Friend and I,
> Across the earth, the sea, the sky.
>
> I do not know what He may be;
> I only know He walks with me.
>
> .   .   .   .   .   .   .   .
> Oh, lonely feet! Oh, bleeding feet!
> In step with mine on the city street![15]

[15] Ralph Cheyney, "Comrade Jesus." Used by permission.

78

# 7

## The Lepers Are Cleansed

WHEN John the Baptist sent from the fortress prison of Machaerus and asked Jesus if he were the Messiah, our Lord's reply, "The blind receive their sight, and the lame walk, the lepers are cleansed" (Matt. 11:5), gives us reason to believe that during his ministry numerous persons afflicted with leprosy were cured by Jesus. We have two specific instances recorded, the account of the cleansing of a leper in Mark 1:40-45 [1] and Luke's record of the healing of ten lepers as found in 17:11-19.

Though leprosy is so rare in our Western civilization that the average physician would not recognize a case if he saw it, still we instinctively shrink when we hear the word. Biblical leprosy does not necessarily involve our disease of this name.[2] Numerous forms of skin afflictions were classified under the general head of leprosy. These would include scrofula or any particularly unsightly skin disorder. This is evident from the fact that the Levitical regulations giving detailed instructions for the priest to pronounce a person cured or clean would be meaningless if the modern disease known as tubercular leprosy was involved (Lev. 13, 14). For the latter there has been no hope of healing until within recent years. At the same time the more virulent form of the disease was certainly indicated in some of the cases. Num. 12:12 speaks of one whose "flesh is half consumed." In

---

[1] Also in Matt. 8:2-4 and Luke 5:12-16.

[2] See Branscomb's adequate treatment in *The Gospel of Mark*, p. 37.

the story of the healing of Naaman (II Kings 5:7) Israel's king thought that the Syrian general was afflicted with an incurable type of leprosy.

Unquestionably in biblical days leprosy was considered to be a symbol of sin. This was due to the disfigurement it involved and the general loathsomeness of the disease. In the very nature of the illness, especially of tubercular leprosy, the patient does not *feel* the sickness, as is ordinarily the case; he *observes* it. His eyes tell him that he is not clean. Other diseases were healed; leprosy was cleansed. The leper was unclean in the same sense that the sinner is unclean. He was cleansed by the same methods: cedar wood, hyssop, scarlet. Leprosy was thought of peculiarly as an affliction sent by God because of some awful sin on the part of the individual or his parents. Leprosy was a living reminder to the Jew of the horror of sin. He could see it and its results with his own eyes. Lepers were forced to live apart. Effective as was quarantine in the control of disease, segregation was enforced on the religious ground of ritual uncleanness on the part of one who had an ulcerous sore, rather than for sanitary reasons. Secondarily, it served to prevent the disease's spreading widely throughout the land. Quarantining is still one of the most effective methods we use for its control.

To the ancient Jew leprosy and sin were almost synonymous. He did not propose to make light of either. In contrast our age has treated sin almost with flippancy—to our own confusion. A sociologist, Harry Elmer Barnes, made probably the most ridiculous statement of this generation when he remarked, "Science teaches us there is no such thing as sin." It is rather significant that he uttered it in the days of the "roaring twenties." Little did he know that the great depression was just around the corner or that World War II was about to plunge our planet into so much agony. We make light of sin, both personal and national, at our peril.

## I. Cleansing of a Leper—*Mark 1:40-45; Matt. 8:2-4; Luke 5:12-16*

During the great Galilean campaign of Jesus a leper pushed through the crowd, knelt down before him, and in a voice mingled with both hope and assurance said, "If thou wilt, thou canst make me clean." Dr. Major holds that this was an exceedingly notable case of healing, probably the first of its kind.[3] It is likewise the first of many stories in which Jesus performs deeds either similar to, or in marked contrast with, those of Elijah and Elisha.

The miracles of healing do not meet with the same degree of disbelief today that is true of some of the nature miracles of Jesus. Medical science is humbler and wiser than it was three decades ago. Dr. Alexis Carrel, one of the greatest scientists and surgeons of our time, in his significant *Man, the Unknown* says:

Prayer may set in motion a strange phenomenon, the miracle. . . . Miraculous cures seldom occur. Despite their small number, they prove the existence of organic and mental processes that we do not know. . . . The most important cases of miraculous healing have been recorded by the Medical Bureau of Lourdes. . . . The miracle is chiefly characterized by an extreme acceleration in the processes of organic repair. There is no doubt that the rate of cicatrization of the anatomical defects is much greater than the normal one. The only condition indispensable to the occurrence of the phenomenon is prayer.[4]

Physicians, along with psychiatrists and psychologists, are quite ready to admit that there is an authenticity about many of the recorded miracles of healing which is not at all improbable in the light of our modern knowledge.

The record tells us that as the leper knelt before Jesus, our Lord was filled with compassion. Most of the miracles were an outgrowth of the tenderness of heart that belonged to Jesus of

[3] See Major, Manson, and Wright, *op. cit.*, p. 48.
[4] Pp. 148-49.

81

Nazareth. They were his method of philanthropy. The outstanding Jewish scholar, C. G. Montefiore, emphasizes this note:

> The leper . . . violated the law, but Jesus before he deals with that
> shows, first of all, compassion. He, too, apparently, violates the
> law . . . as he touches the man in order to heal him. Here we begin to
> catch a new note in the ministry of Jesus: his intense compassion for
> the outcast, the sufferer who, by his sin, or by his suffering, found
> himself rejected and despised by man and believed himself rejected
> and despised by God. Here was a new and lofty note, new and
> exquisite manifestation of the very pity and love which the prophets
> had demanded. [5]

An endearing name that we sometimes use of Jesus today is
Great Physician. For many there is genuine religious value in the
old gospel hymn:

> The great Physician now is near,
> The sympathizing Jesus;
> He speaks the drooping heart to cheer,
> Oh, hear the voice of Jesus.
>
> Sweetest note in seraph song,
> Sweetest name on mortal tongue;
> Sweetest carol ever sung,
> Jesus, blessed Jesus.

Strangely enough, the leper said, "*If thou wilt*, thou canst
make me clean." He was fully persuaded of the power of Jesus;
he was not sure of his willingness. In all likelihood this was an
outgrowth of the popular view that leprosy was due to sin. The
leper was not certain whether a man with the personal integrity
of Jesus would care to have any dealings with one who bore in
his body the living symbol of God's curse. Today none would
question the willingness of Jesus, even though some might question his power. In all likelihood the leper himself believed that his
disease was due to some sin he had committed, knowingly or even

[5] *Op. cit.*, I, 39.

unknowingly. The poor fellow had likely wracked his brain on more than one occasion to find just what incident it was in his life in which he had transgressed to such a degree that God had brought upon him this awful scourge.

With quiet deliberateness and generosity of heart our Lord reached out his hand and touched the poor fellow as he said, "I will; be thou clean." The touch of a leper made one unclean ceremonially. His close proximity endangered everyone in the crowd. This was probably the reason that Jesus used the strong words, "Be off.⁶ Show yourself to the priest," just after he had effected the cure. Intent upon his own crying needs, the leper had disregarded the regulations that should have made him ask for healing from a distance and had pushed thoughtlessly into the crowd. Jesus did not hesitate to break the ceremonial law by touching the leper himself.

Whether Jesus felt that this man's malady was due to sin we are not told. We do know that our Lord on other occasions pointed out specifically that there was no connection between disability and sin. "Neither hath this man sinned, nor his parents: but that the works of God should be made manifest in him." (John 9:3.) Here Jesus went counter to the accepted position of his day. The up-to-dateness of his viewpoint in this, as in so many other factors, is quite marked. Jesus did feel that he had power over both sickness and sin. There was an urgent reality about both to his sensitive nature. The Son of man had come to usher in God's order, in which most sickness ought to be as foreign as sin, for he believed that God wills health and wholeness for his children. Whether it was a case of sickness or of sin, Jesus knew that he had power from his heavenly Father to overcome it.

Christians are not far amiss in thinking that the purity of Jesus was such that instead of being contaminated, he made clean. In verse 41 some manuscripts read, "Moved with anger,"

---

⁶ ὕπαγε.

rather than, "Moved with compassion." Should this be correct, the "anger" was certainly directed against the unseen power of evil which occasioned the pitiable state of the leper rather than against the man himself.[7] Along with the injunction to show himself to the priest, Jesus told the man to keep what had happened to himself. Legally the leper was still unclean until the priest, as the local health officer, had given him what we would term a clean bill of health.

Jesus had to caution against publishing abroad the healing. This was necessary because the Master knew that his ministry was primarily a ministry of preaching and only secondarily one of healing. The man disregarded the injunction of Jesus and broadcast the account of his cure. The very exuberance of his new-found health made it hard for him to keep to himself the name of the one who had brought restoration. Just as he feared, Jesus had to cease his ministry of preaching because of the excitement aroused by the news of the cure. The crowd comprised both those seeking healing and others who out of curiosity wanted to observe the new rabbi "pass a miracle." Jesus' primary mission was the cure of souls. We might call it his vocation. On the other hand, his avocation which grew out of his sympathetic and compassionate nature, was the care for bodies. The Church today is rightly concerned about its social obligations, but it would be wise, as did its great Founder, to keep primary those things that are primary.

Early-church Christians had experienced in their souls cleansing from the malady of sin. They remembered this story with vividness and recounted it with gladness. Our generation is suffering from mortal soul sickness that is as destructive to human relations as leprosy has ever been to the individual. *Time* magazine, in commenting on the installation of the president of a

---

[7] Goguel holds that he was a healed leper who had not been ritually purified. This gave Jesus an opportunity to show, early in his ministry, that he was not setting his authority against that of the Jerusalem temple leaders (*Life of Jesus*, p. 300).

world-famous technical school, which was attended by many internationally-known speakers on politics and science, said:

Most of the speakers . . . agreed that man's chief task in these times was not how to harness nature in order to stay alive, but how to harness himself. His problem was moral—how to order his life. That problem was not peculiar to the 20th Century; but 20th Century scientific progress had given it a dreadful urgency. [8]

Not often do we look to political leaders for spiritual guidance, but during this mid-century convocation Winston Churchill, in one of the most moving addresses of his great career, recognized that our pride had become our downfall. He said, "We read in the Bible—you do read the Bible, don't you?—'Jeshurun waxed fat, and kicked.' " As he diagnosed international ills correctly, so he provided the right remedy for our malady:

The flame of Christian ethics is still our highest guide. To guard and cherish it is our first interest, both spiritually and materially. The fulfillment of spiritual duty in our daily life is vital to our survival. . . . Let us then move forward together, . . . fearing God and nothing else.

Modern man, in his insufferable pride, has rebelled against the biblical truth that we have all sinned and fallen short of the glory of God. Yet while we have rebelled, the greatest of sins have come upon us—Dachau, Buchenwald, Hiroshima. An encouraging factor is that we have an uneasy conscience. Americans may feel that dropping the atomic bomb was a military necessity, but nearly every time it is referred to in print, there is a note of contrition. Like the leper we wonder if God will really forgive us. Though we have more and better science, more and better education, and more and better productive capacity, we do not yet have more righteousness, and so all of the above threatens to destroy us. We too need to be made clean.

The leper knew that above all things he needed cleansing.

[8] April 11, 1949, p. 27.

Not until we recognize our own need to be made whole in spirit, as well as body, is there much hope for us. Although modern man does not have a sense of sin, he has a kind of moralistic substitute that often becomes psychopathic and has contributed so much to the disillusionment and cynicism of our time. Because modern man so often has no conscience of sin against God, because he has no God, he has no saving secret for dealing with his moral failure. A wholesome sense of sin which can lead to forgiveness is unconsciously repressed until it becomes a morbid complex.[9] Even those of us who by all the external standards are living as we should, if we are morally earnest know that we too have failed.

> I never cut my neighbor's throat;
> My neighbor's gold I never stole;
> I never spoiled his house and land;
> *But God have mercy on my soul!*
>
> For I am haunted night and day
> By all the deeds I have not done;
> O unattempted loveliness!
> O costly valor never won! [10]

Hope for the leper lay in the hands of Jesus. He knew his need and went to the only one in that day who could give help. The one horizon of hope for our mortally unclean generation is that we too are recognizing that it is only by the precepts and ideals which Jesus of Nazareth came to give men that we can expect even a modicum of peace on earth, to say nothing of good will toward men.

## II. THE TEN LEPERS—*Luke 17:11-19*

Luke gives us the other specific healing of leprosy that is recorded in the Gospels. His is the Gospel par excellence for the

[9] D. M. Baillie, *God Was in Christ*, p. 166.
[10] Marguerite Wilkinson, "Guilty." Used by permission.

foreigner, the Gentile. Luke's emphasis was ever upon the graciousness of our Lord when it came to those who were not Israelites. When his disciples wanted Jesus to play the part of Elijah and call fire from heaven on a group of surly Samaritans, the response was a rebuke for their spiritual blindness (9:52-56). Luke is the one who preserves the parable of the good Samaritan. Here is another record of a Samaritan who showed more spiritual understanding than did his Jewish companions.

There is some ambiguity in the eleventh verse. It is likely that Jesus was traveling toward the east, along the border of Galilee and Samaria. This explanation gives an adequate background for the joint community of ten lepers, one of whom was a Samaritan.

How misery loves company! This Samaritan leper was accepted by his nine Jewish fellow sufferers. Had they all been well, the Jews and the Samaritan would have had no dealings with each other. Their mutual personal tragedy gave them a tolerance plus an understanding which they would not have possessed otherwise. Often it takes tragedy to bring people together. In contrast with the cleansing of the leper, as recorded by Mark, these ten men were very meticulous about the health regulations. Luke, as the physician-author, seems interested in recording this fact. They stood afar off and cried out saying, "Jesus, Master, have mercy on us." Jesus, evidently at some distance, said unto them, "Go shew yourselves unto the priests."

In both instances Jesus abode by the letter of the law, which demanded that a leper be pronounced clean by the priest, who had responsibility for the health of the community.[11] As the ten turned away from Jesus, did their thoughts parallel those of Naaman in the Old Testament story? Surely this great healer

[11] Creed, *op. cit.*, p. 216, feels that this is sufficient evidence to believe the account in Luke is an idealized version of Mark's healing. However, the only things in common are a similar malady and the injunction to go to the priest. The application is entirely different.

and teacher ought to speak an incantation or make a sign or two and immediately they would see the visible results in their whited bodies. But no, he rather commanded them to start their journey to the priest just as if they were whole. Action involved a degree of faith on their part. On the way each one experienced the tingling of life sensation coming back into his wasted body, the flesh slowly becoming firm and sweet and fresh. Steinmeyer has an interesting exposition of the reason for the gradual cleansing as they were on their way to the priests.

The matter becomes plain, if we think on the spiritual effects which the Lord wished to symbolize by these miracles. In fact, the cleansing from sinful habits, which is accomplished by the grace of Christ, is by no means perfected immediately; it is a gradual work, it happens "as one goes." The *forgiveness* of sins can be embraced by faith and taken immediate possession of; the *purification* from sinful works is a gradual work. . . . The nine gave no proof that they had become clean in a higher sense, as they were contaminated immediately by a pagan vice—ingratitude." [12]

As in the story of the other Samaritan, whose compassion caused him to help one in need on the Jericho road, this Samaritan had a far greater understanding of true spiritual reality than his Jewish companions. The record says that the Samaritan leper gave glory to God for his healing. Along with the other nine, he believed that Jesus, the prophet and healer from Galilee, could do something about his situation. Yet he knew that the ultimate power was from God, and so with shouts and rejoicing he ascribed to God the honor. He had put his faith in the highest, and that faith was rewarded, not only by the healing of his body, but also by the far more wonderful healing of his soul. Jesus asked the rhetorical question, "Were there not ten cleansed? but where are the nine? There are not found that returned to give glory to God, save this stranger." He immediately followed with a glad, "Arise, go thy way: thy faith hath made thee

[12] *The Miracles of Our Lord*, p. 100.

whole." The leper's trust in Jesus as God's representative had won him cleansing from the scourge in his body. His gratitude to God, who had shown such power through Jesus, now won him freedom from the greater leprosy of sin. He knew the grace of gratitude; he had found what it means to love God as he had seen him in Jesus.

Once the son of the great Bishop Berkeley asked his father what was the difference between the cherubim and the seraphim. His learned and good father replied that the word "cherubim" came from a Hebrew word signifying knowledge, and that "seraphim" came from a Hebrew word meaning burning, from which the theologians have inferred that the cherubim were spirits famed for their knowledge, while the seraphim were famed for their burning love. It is said that the boy replied to his father, "I hope when I die I shall be a seraph, for I would rather love God than know all things." Exactly, that is what the grateful leper discovered when he returned to Jesus, in whose face he had seen the glory.

The spirit of the Christ who could heal the leper has so permeated the hearts of many men that they have been challenged by his goodness to serve others with all of the strength of their endeavor. Some have even been willing to become lepers if by this means they could win lepers to a knowledge of God as seen in Christ Jesus our Lord. The classic instance of our time is that of Father Damien. A young Belgian who was ordained a priest at twenty-three, Damien went as a missionary to the South Sea. Nine years later he volunteered for duty among the lepers of Molokai. With somewhat of the passion of our Lord, Father Damien made this his great work. The turning point in his life came when he was forty-five. It was on a hot Sunday in June, 1885, when he failed to begin his sermon with the usual salutation, "My brethren," but opened with the grim and compassionate words, "We lepers." Damien died three years later. Robert Louis Stevenson made famous his living sacrifice in a letter that has become a classic. People around the world have never ceased to wonder at the challenge Christ could bring to a man so that he would be willing to give himself to this degree. Damien had learned from one who testified that among the proofs of his divine ministry was, "The lepers are cleansed."

# 8

## Children Jesus Healed

When I was sick and lay abed,
I had two pillows at my head,
And all my toys beside me lay
To keep me happy all the day.

And sometimes for an hour or so
I watched my leaden soldiers go,
With different uniforms and drills,
Among the bed clothes, through the hills;

And sometimes sent my ships in fleets
All up and down among the sheets;
Or brought my trees and houses out,
And planted cities all about.

I was a giant great and still
That sits upon the pillow-hill,
And sees before him, dale and plain,
The pleasant land of counterpane. [1]

Do YOU remember Robert Louis Stevenson writing about a sick lad? There is always something wistfully appealing about sick children. They are helpless, pitiful, and utterly dependent; one's heart always goes out in a sympathetic desire to help in some way. Matthew paints a true picture of Jesus when he records the words of our Lord, "Suffer little children, and forbid

[1] Robert Louis Stevenson, "The Land of Counterpane." Used by permission Charles Scribner's Sons, publisher.

them not, to come unto me: for of such is the kingdom of heaven." Though Jesus never had children of his own, this is an attitude that we expect of him. His universal heart was warmed by the happy laughter of little children. It would be very remarkable if in the gospel records, in which so many of his deeds of mercy and kindness are recorded, there were no accounts of his healing of children.

## I. THE NOBLEMAN'S SON—*John 4:46-54*

The first of the three instances in which Jesus brought recovery to a child is that of the nobleman's son, as found in John. The two accounts of the restoration to life of Jairus' daughter and the widow of Nain's son will be discussed later. Many scholars see the account of the nobleman's son as a free rendering of the synoptic incident of the healing of the centurion's servant at Capernaum (Matt. 8:5-13; Luke 7:1-10). However, there is no reason to regard this as necessary, for there are marked differences in the two stories.[2] Both accounts do have healing at a distance, and there is persistence of entreaty which is rewarded, but otherwise the differences are striking.

Matthew and Luke speak of a "boy" as we would call a "boy" to take our bags at the station. Both say that he was a slave. The record in John concerns a son. The officer in the Synoptic Gospels is a centurion. John tells us that a "king's officer" went to find Jesus; "nobleman" is a poor translation. Some have thought that this was Chuza, Herod's steward (Luke 8:3). Others think it was Manaen (Acts 13:1). But both names are suggested only because they are mentioned in the New Testament. The king's officer finds Jesus at Cana, not Capernaum. The towns were twenty miles apart; the lad was sick at Capernaum. In any event, the father with anguish comes to Jesus and asks that his lad may be healed. Here the boy is definitely his son. Possibly the child had infantile paralysis, for a fever is usually connected

[2] So Garvie in the *Abingdon Bible Commentary*, p. 1072; Major, Manson, and Wright, *op. cit.*, p. 751. For the opposite view see Bernard, *op. cit.*, p. 166.

with this malady, and the swiftness of its attack and the general helplessness in the face of it baffle even modern medical science.

Jesus replies with what seems to be a harsh statement to this man's plea for his son, "Except ye see signs and wonders, ye will not believe." The whole tenor of the ministry of Jesus forces us to conclude that there was a purpose in these strange and apparently difficult words, for he did bring recovery to the lad. The insistence of the father that Jesus "come down" gives a clue. Like so many of his day, he was evidently a believer in magical healing. The father felt that it was necessary for Jesus to be present before his boy could be cured. He would have to utter an incantation in the presence of the sick person in order to effect a cure. We recall that a somewhat similar belief is found in connection with the healing of Naaman (II Kings 5: 1-14). The differences between this king's officer and the centurion are so striking that Augustine drew a sharp contrast between the faith of the centurion and the unbelief of the nobleman.[3] Is not the account evidence that the father in his own mind thought of the power of Jesus as limited? Another factor may be that Jesus hesitated to begin in Galilee a ministry that had disappointed him so in Judea (John 2:23-25).

Then John's purpose was to show the value of faith apart from the presence of Jesus. "Blessed are they that have not seen, and yet have believed." Our Lord knew that the best proof of his relation to God was not necessarily his miracles, but his whole gracious personality. So Jesus in this statement implies a condemnation of faith that is dependent on miracle. Jesus was a man of his own day and generation, yet his insights continually make us exclaim, "What a modern mind he had!" He seems aware that a day would come when miracle, instead of proving a bulwark of faith, would become a stumbling block to a scientific age. Nevertheless, here was need looming large and insistent, and the relief of human need was the very life and breath of the one from God.

[3] *In Joannis Evangelium* 16.

At this point, with anguished insistence, the father commands action. "Come down ere my child die!" To the father it is not faith that matters; it is action. After listening to the symptoms Jesus with calm assurance gave hope to the father, "Go thy way; thy son liveth." [4] No matter how minute or imperfect was the faith, Jesus could never resist a cry for help. The father made a mental note of the time. It was the seventh hour, one P.M. "The man believed the word that Jesus had spoken unto him." He had asked for the presence of Jesus by the bedside of the son he felt to be dying. It would be a long journey—the father himself did not arrive until the next day—but the words of Jesus carried such self-authenticating hope that the king's officer turned and started for home. The interesting mental note of the father about the time of day the words of Jesus were spoken is either an indication of a still lingering doubt on his part or perfect assurance of healing. As John always sees the beginning of an incident in the light of its ending, the latter is the interpretation the author evidently put upon the situation.

To his joy the father was met on the way by retainers who advised him that the lad was well on the way to recovery. On checking with the servants, he observed that the boy began to mend at the very hour when Jesus had told him that his son lived. Certainly the father thought a miracle had been performed. The record goes on to say that he and his whole house believed. Not only had they experienced the power of Jesus, but now they knew something about the reality of faith in Jesus. Notice what has taken place: A father had received an enlarged faith. God's power was manifested through Jesus whether he was present or not—that is the lesson John is especially underlining. Added to this fact a whole household was drawn closer

[4] Some commentators have felt that no miracle was intended. Jesus, from a review of the symptoms, believed that the lad would recover. He is only represented as saying, "Thy son liveth," that is, "He will recover." Even with modern expert medical diagnosis it would be a rash physician who would give an opinion at a distance. Such a view simply transforms the incident from a miracle of healing to one of superhuman knowledge.

94

together through the alchemy of suffering. In the light of our fuller understanding of what our Lord is to men and households we would certainly say that from that time on Jesus was the unseen Friend of that home.

It was a case we would today classify as "telepathic healing." Modern psychical research is beginning to establish a scientific basis for the possibility of such healing. [5] Just what took place, of course, we do not know. Dr. Wright has some pertinent observations on this passage: Jesus did cure folks by means that we would not classify as usual medical procedure. Such healings have been related in many ages and among different peoples.

The explanation is to be sought in the realm of the unexplored potencies of the spirit and of its actions on the body. In the case of Jesus, that potency, operating in accord with psychical laws which are to us yet obscure, was very remarkable. These healings must not be regarded as "miracles" in the old sense of that much used, and much abused, word; that is, they are not, of necessity, events which by their very nature are incapable of subsumption under law. We are not living in a magical universe. No event is, as we believe, without its antecedent causative factors. It is the business of science to discover these factors, and to employ the knowledge so gained in the interest of maimed and sick humanity. [6]

Jesus did possess unusual spiritual power. It was spiritual power of such a quality that it had to flow to the place of human need wherever there was faith which, like a syphon, would make its transference possible. The requisites for the release of this power were: first, human need; second, belief in the power of Jesus' personality as adequate to fill the need; third, faith in the goodness of God. When these three tests are applied to our present world situation, we see that Jesus is the only one adequate to our present need, but he is! The philosopher-statesman Jan Christian Smuts never wrote more truly than when he said,

[5] Rudolph Otto has an interesting discussion of this incident in his *Kingdom of God and the Son of Man*, p. 350.

[6] Major, Manson, and Wright, *op. cit.*, p. 752.

"Fundamentally the world has no need of a new order or a new plan but only of an honest and courageous application of the historic Christian idea."

## II. DAUGHTER OF THE SYROPHOENICIAN WOMAN—*Mark 7:24-30; Matt. 15:21-28*

Only in our day and among Western people has the birth of a girl baby brought the same joy as a man child. But when children wrap themselves about heartstrings, it never has mattered whether they were boys or girls.

Mark's account of the healing of the Syrophoenician woman's daughter is paralleled in Matthew. It is unusual to find Jesus in a typical Gentile or foreign area. The record says that Jesus went into the "coasts of Tyre and Sidon," and the impression is that it was a journey of some duration. Tyre is just west of the northern border of Galilee, and Sidon some thirty miles farther north, on the Syrian coast. Jesus was hounded by Herod, who was seeking his life. The tension of the Galilean situation had become such that Jesus thought it best to retire for a while from the opposition of ecclesiastical and political leaders. This excursion into Gentile territory may have been occasioned simply for the quiet and the privacy that our Lord needed at this time in his ministry. Mark states that he wanted to keep his presence in the house a secret. The whole story is evidence that he had not entered upon an evangelistic tour of this area.

However, this woman whose daughter was ill heard that the Jewish rabbi whose healings had brought such a blessing to multitudes of homes in Galilee was now in her town. She sought out Jesus and pleaded with him that her daughter might be healed. Though Gentiles felt cruelly the superiority so tacitly assumed by the Jews, the illness of her daughter rose above any difference in race. Humanity is one, and if a Jewish healer could cure her sick child, what matter race? Christ is breaking down the middle wall of partition that has separated race from race.

The fine Negro poet Countee Cullen well put it in his "Simon the Cyrenian Speaks":

> At first I said, "I will not bear
> His cross upon my back;
> He only seeks to place it there
> Because my skin is black."
>
> .    .    .    .    .    .
>
> It was Himself my pity bought;
> I did for Christ alone
> What all of Rome could not have wrought
> With bruise of lash or stone. [7]

During Detroit's terrible race riots of 1943 I was pastor of the First Baptist Church there. Driving downtown early Monday morning I was all unconscious that a riot was in progress until I saw with my own eyes cars burning and men being beaten. One of the incidents indelibly fixed in my mind involved a Catholic priest who was endeavoring to protect a Negro family, but was shouldered aside by a rioter who said, "I'm a religious man too, but this situation has got to the place where religion won't solve it!" Of course, the answer is that if religion will not solve it, nothing will.

This woman was a Greek speaking Syrophoenician. There is every likelihood that Jesus carried on the conversation in the common Greek language of his day, the Koine. It would have been very remarkable if he had not been bilingual, having been raised in Galilee. This is true, though the bulk of his ministry was conducted normally in his native tongue.

With a tinge of human dismay Jesus saw what would happen if a major healing was accomplished. He had come here for privacy, and he knew that there would be none if the request was granted. How often and how thoughtlessly those whom he blessed with his healing ministry and counseled to remain quiet shouted it from the housetops. They publicized a philanthropy

[7] From *Color*. Copyright 1925 by Harper & Bros. Used by permission.

Jesus would much have preferred to have been kept in secret. His primary ministry was to the spirit, and cures that were noised abroad occasioned thronging that made his principal task more difficult. In this particular situation there was the added problem of his own personal safety. If Herod Antipas was seeking his life, Jesus as a fugitive could have been turned over to him. Mark states that Jesus did not wish his whereabouts disclosed at this time. All of the above may have a bearing on what follows.

With apparent brusqueness Jesus replies to her earnest entreaty, "Let the children first be filled: for it is not meet to take the children's bread, and to cast it unto the dogs." Given the whole character of Jesus and the final outcome, some interpreters see his harshness as assumed and the whole incident an acted parable to convince the disciples that the heathen too might have faith and a part in the blessings reserved for the true followers of God. Matthew adds that Jesus remarked, "I am not sent but unto the lost sheep of the house of Israel." He was Jewish to the core. He was sent to Israel; he could win the world only as he first gained a sure footing among his own people. Like the prophets of old, he gave his message first to those with his own Jewish background. "He lived in a world in which the presuppositions of thought of Palentinian Jews and the neighboring Gentiles were so basically different that it was virtually out of the question for one to serve both peoples." [8] Sholem Asch, in both his *Nazarene* and *Apostle*, vividly and accurately contrasts life among pagans with that in "the blessed land of Israel."

Matthew has the woman address Jesus as "thou son of David." This gives the possibility of an alternative suggestion, according to an interesting interpretation of Shafto:

In Matthew the woman called Him "Son of David," and Jesus desired to show her that she had no right of approach if that was really all that she thought of him; but if he stood to her for a love

_____
[8] Branscomb, *op. cit.*, p. 131.

that knows no limits, racial or other, if he was her "Lord" and not a mere wonder-worker of another nationality, then she, too, had her place and her lawful claim upon his ministry. [9]

The parable of the good Samaritan is the best commentary on any apparent exclusiveness.

Another factor must be considered in connection with this incident. We need to remember that if, as the book of Hebrews says, our Lord learned obedience by the things that he suffered, he also learned largeness of heart out of the life situations which he faced. He did not cease increasing "in wisdom and stature, and in favour with God and man" as a boy of twelve. Here is a splendid example. The person trained in a background of exclusiveness—and this was true of Jesus as of all Jews of his day—tends to think in generalities. His mental process is one of going from the whole to the particular: all Gentiles are outside the pale of God's love and care; all Chinese are queer; all conservatives are narrow; all liberals are Unitarians; all Negroes are ignorant. Therefore this Gentile has no claim on God, or this Negro is ignorant. The fallacy is obvious once one knows a specific Gentile or a specific Negro. For instance, C. J. Daniels, who for twenty-eight years was secretary of Virginia State College, at Petersburg, has four sons who hold the Ph.D. degree. Two of these degrees were granted by the University of Chicago and two by Columbia University. The Danielses are Baptists and Negroes. I know of no other family in Baptist circles, Negro or white, in which there are four sons with Ph.D. degrees from such outstanding educational institutions.

The big, and the broad, and the good man, no matter what his training has been, learns to go, not from the whole to the particular, but from the particular to the whole. There was a definite greatening of Abraham Lincoln under the stress of the Civil War. It is biblical, and not heretical, to hold that the largeness of our Lord was influenced by such situations as this. See

[9] *Wonders of the Kingdom,* p. 70.

the progression: "I am not sent but unto the lost sheep of the house of Israel. . . . O woman, great is thy faith: be it unto thee even as thou wilt." Of another Gentile, Jesus said, "I have not found so great faith, no, not in Israel." And finally we have his inclusive "Come unto me, *all* ye that labour." Here is evidence of a complete cycle: anyone different from me and my group is wrong, but this particular person surely has a claim on God's mercy and power; therefore, "Come unto me, *all* ye that labour." And, "Go ye therefore, and teach *all* nations."

The very preservation of the harsh words is one of the best proofs that they are authentic and represent a true reflection of the mind of Jesus in this particular situation. Claude Montefiore, the great Jewish scholar, is fascinated by this story. Its naturalness and the reality of the one behind it are plain to him.

The story is one of great beauty and charm. Whence this wonderful attractiveness of so much of the gospel narrative, this marvelous combination of power and simplicity? Whence this impression of *first-classness*, of inspiration? Surely because the gospels are the early result of the impression produced by a great and inspired personality. . . . Only a real Jesus could have caused the Gospel. Without Jesus, no Mark. [10]

If the woman's request were granted, the ministry he had been forced by circumstances to deny to his own people would now be bestowed upon Gentiles. Branscomb suggests [11] that his words are not so much an answer to the request of the woman as an evidence of his own feeling over the crucial issue which he faced. The harshness is directed to his own problems, rather than being an insult to the woman. The development of the story probably gives a clue as adequate as any.

The whole conversation was carried on with a smile and a whimsical raillery which show the humanness of this strong man from Galilee. It is certain that he was fascinated by the

[10] *Op. cit.,* I, 169.
[11] *Op. cit.,* p. 132.

quickness of wit, born of her desperation and concern for her daughter, as she said, "Truth, Lord: yet the dogs [the little house pets] eat of the crumbs." The word "dog" used in the conversation is not the Eastern pariah dog, but a small house pet, so there is no sting in the word. She matched proverb with proverb. Her readiness in retort, no less than her faith, as Bruce well said, "gave him exquisite delight." [12] With chivalrous humor Jesus granted her request. Her daughter was healed.

In this case, as in that of the nobleman's son, Jesus did not see the child who was the recipient of his blessed healing ministry. He did not need to. His consecrated imagination was such and his sympathy was such that his heart went out to them anyway. When our children are sick and suffering, is it too much to believe that Jesus cares?

> O yes, He cares; I know He cares,
>   His heart is touched with my grief;
> When the days are weary, the long nights dreary,
>   I know my Savior cares. [13]

## III. THE EPILEPTIC BOY—*Mark 9:14-29; Matt. 17:14-20; Luke 9:37-43*

An entirely different situation faces us in the poignant instance of the healing of an afflicted lad at the foot of the Mount of Transfiguration. Of the three instances this is the only one in which Jesus actually saw the need with his own eyes. Here we find one of the most vivid of gospel scenes. There is a realism about the incident which makes us see it with full graphic clearness. Mark's use of detail and the vividness of his account are apparent. The more literary Matthew and Luke omit some of Mark's detail, which they considered unimportant. Here is excellent instance of evidence for an eyewitness; for though a writer of artistry might have invented incidents that give color,

[12] *Op. cit.*, p. 263.
[13] Copyright 1929. Renewal. The Rodeheaver Co., owner. Used by permission.

they evidently passed over these as not being worth recording. In passing it might be remarked that Jesus was the only one who was completely at ease in both situations. One group of disciples did not know what to do on the Mount, and the others were powerless to help in the valley.

A distracted father had brought his epileptic son to the disciples. Matthew describes him as "moon-struck." The father had enough faith to believe that the followers of Jesus ought to be able to bring help in his situation. How often needy humanity comes to those of us who walk after the Nazarene, and we fail utterly through some lack. The rebuke, "O faithless and perverse generation" is typical of that of the prophets and is directed as much to the crowd as to the disciples. It has been pointed out that the language of Mark is such that the disciples may not have even tried to effect a cure.[14] They were powerless when they ought to have been mighty, for they had experience with exorcisms, and the father certainly thought they should be able to help his son. When asked later why the disciples could not effect a cure, Jesus answered, "This kind can come forth by nothing, but by prayer." This holds true for modern Christians as well as ancient disciples.

As a good physician Jesus began to get the case history from the father. "How long is it ago since this came unto him?" And he said, "Of a child. And ofttimes it hath cast him into the fire, and into the waters, to destroy him: but if thou canst do any thing, have compassion on us, and help us." With vehemence Jesus replied, "If thou canst!" A paraphrase would be, "If I can! All things are possible to me, because I believe in God, and all things will be possible to you if you only believe." In agonizing earnestness the father cried out, "I believe; help thou mine unbelief." It is a noble cry from a desperate man. Just at this moment the boy had a seizure. In the intensity of the lad's crisis Jesus said, "Thou dumb and deaf spirit, I charge thee, come

[14] T. H. Robinson, *The Gospel of Matthew* ("Moffatt New Testament Commentary"), p. 148.

102

out of him, and enter no more into him." He is here using the technical word for exorcism. The boy was shaken by a series of convulsions which seemed to leave him lifeless. But Jesus took him by the hand, raised him up, and delivered him to his father.

The epileptic boy was healed, not because of his own faith, but because of the faith of his father and the abounding faith of Jesus in his power over all demon possessions. To the inquiry of the disciples later as to why they could not effect a cure, Jesus said that only by prayer can such a one be healed. Matthew adds a homily on faith, "If ye have faith as a grain of mustard seed, ye shall say unto this mountain, Remove hence to yonder place; and it shall remove; and nothing shall be impossible unto you."

Jesus had the faith, and he was a man mighty in prayer, Lord of every situation. Whether on the Mount of Transfiguration or in the valley of need, our Lord knew exactly what to do. In Steinbeck's play *The Moon Is Down*, Mayor Orden is held a prisoner by the enemy, who bring cruel pressure upon him. Finally his friends advise him to give up his resistance. He answers with the thrilling words, "They elected me not to be confused." The people of the village had given him high office because they trusted that he would be calm in a crisis. Jesus knew no confusion in the glory of his experience with Moses and Elijah on the Mount, nor was he baffled by the demon of epilepsy in the valley, but "this kind can come forth by nothing, but by prayer."

# 9

## Women Jesus Healed

I THANK Thee that I was not born a dog; I thank Thee that I was not born a Gentile; I thank Thee that I was not born a woman."

One is shocked to read this notorious rabbinic prayer that comes down to us from the first century. While it is not typical, the fact that it has been preserved shows that it expresses a viewpoint all too prevalent in that day. The study of the status of women through the centuries is a revealing experience indeed. The development of the rights of human personality goes hand in hand with the rights of women. Almost from the beginning the Jewish people had a far higher regard for their women than did the people of their time. Yet it is true that the emancipation of woman began with Jesus. In the gospel records there are three instances in which our Lord specifically healed women. There are the same elements of high tenderness in these accounts that we find in his other relations with women.

I. THE MOTHER OF SIMON PETER'S WIFE—*Mark 1:29-31; Matt. 8:14-15; Luke 4:38-39*

The first of these instances of healing is that in connection with Simon Peter's mother-in-law. The worship services in the synagogue had been a particularly busy time for Jesus, because during the service he exorcised a demon. Immediately after he and a group of friends repaired to the home of his new-found disciple, Simon, for food and rest. We should beware of drawing a parallel with the modern custom of a heavy Sunday meal. Food on the Jewish Sabbath was never elaborate. Most of it had been prepared on the previous day. It was designed simply to provide necessary nourishment. While the other members of the household worshiped in the synagogue, Peter's mother-in-law remained at home. Evidently between the time when Peter left for the service and his return with Jesus she was taken quite ill.

Mother-in-law stories are products of our time. It was as natural for the mother of Peter's wife to live in his home as for the wife to be there. There is every indication that she filled her place in that home with peace and helpfulness. Peter, like the rest of the twelve, was a married man; for to the Hebrew, marriage was an honorable estate, blessed by God and established for the happiness and well-being of all men, priest and people alike.

The woman's difficulty can only be conjectured. Luke terms it "a great fever." It came upon her suddenly and departed as quickly. This suggests the possibility of malaria, which was a common malady in a lakeside town. There is a certain disease of which the Talmud speaks in the same technical terms. It prescribes a magical remedy: on successive days tie a knife by a braid of hair to a thorn bush, and then at the end of the treatment cut the bush down, and the patient will be healed!

This instance of healing is of especial interest for a number of reasons. It is one of the first recorded healing miracles. Keim says that it carries a power of conviction like no other.[1] The incident in itself is not too striking. No effort is made to paint the illness as something quite serious. The one who originally recorded the story certainly showed no morbid love of the marvelous. Peter's mother-in-law had been apparently well shortly before and, in all probability, would have speedily been restored in the normal course of human events.

From the standpoint of modern New Testament investigation

[1] *Jesu von Nazara*, II, 220.

this miracle story is of particular interest because of the almost perfect "form" it takes. The patient is introduced, her illness is named, and Jesus is made aware of the situation. Our Lord takes the hand of the sick person and raises her up. The cure is announced, and it is pointed out that the healing was so complete that the patient was able to wait on the guests. There is also a homily implied in the whole story: the Christian who had been freed from the grip of sin and restored to health ought to use the new-found strength in the service of the Lord.[2]

When Jesus entered the home and saw the condition, he immediately responded to the human need. Luke the physician tells us "he stood over her"—in a truly professional manner. Mark says he "took her by the hand." Then Luke tells us he "rebuked the fever." Here we have the technical word for the exorcising of a demon, but the whole incident shows the lack of any magic in our Lord's method. He was quiet, helpful, and completely confident. It is a known medical fact that bodily temperatures are affected by the nervous condition of the patient. Dr. Hadfield has reported a change of over twenty degrees registered by the thermometer in a patient's hand, occurring in some twenty minutes, which was due solely to repeated suggestions to the patient—not under hypnosis—of a gradually rising temperature. So Luke's description of a cure achieved by "rebuke" or, to follow Dr. Hadfield, by telling the temperature to go down" may not be so unscientific after all.[3] Luke is particularly interested in the immediacy of the cure, although all three evangelists say that she ministered unto them. It was a cure, not a convalescence.

As simple as was the whole incident, it made a very profound impression on the people of the village, for that evening, after the close of the Sabbath, they brought a great multitude of their

[2] See Trench, *op. cit.*, p. 251; Alan Richardson, *Miracle Stories of the Gospels*, p. 76.

[3] Shafto, *op. cit.*, p. 115.

sick to be healed.[4] The teaching which the early Christians could especially appreciate involves the thought of being "saved to serve," a slogan that has been popularized in our day. On numerous occasions Jesus coupled the matter of spiritual and material benefits with the necessity for effective service to others. As Jesus had ministered to her in curing the fever, so she was now happy to serve him.

Lord of the pots and pipkins, since I have no time to be
A saint by doing lovely things and vigilling with Thee,
By watching in the twilight dawn, and storming Heaven's gates,
Make me a saint by getting meals and washing up the plates.[5]

## II. STRAIGHTENING OF THE HUNCHBACKED WOMAN—*Luke 13: 10-17*

Luke alone gives us the story of the hunchbacked woman "whom Satan hath bound, lo, these eighteen years." There are evidences here of a physiopsychic cause for her condition. The words "whom Satan hath bound" would give some indication of a nervous origin. Whatever the cause of her difficulty, the poor woman was seeking spiritual strength in the house of God. The crippled, twisted, and deformed have always had hard burdens to bear. Their physical handicap is grievous enough, but the psychical problem for them and those with whom they come in contact is often even more severe. In biblical days only the physically perfect "without a blemish" could serve God in many capacities (Lev. 21:17). It is encouraging that in our day, when we are beginning to take maiming or deformity as a fact of life that should be accepted as casually as the color of one's hair, medical science is doing such wonders in straightening backs by spinal fusion as well as performing other marvels of bone surgery. It was not so in the days of Jesus. He and the

[4] "Keim regards the healing of the demoniac in the synagogue as unhistorical and, therefore, is obliged to ascribe the excitement in Capernaum not to it but to what happened in Peter's home" (Bruce, *op. cit.*, p. 156).
[5] From Cecily Hallack, "The Divine Office of the Kitchen."

evangelist may have felt that Satan had bound this poor woman, but to most of the congregation some dire iniquity on her part lay back of it. In their minds sickness, deformity, and sin were intimately connected. This is a view that is still held in some circles. Jesus definitely rejected such a theology. "Neither hath this man sinned, nor his parents." We know, and Jesus helped us to understand, that sickness or maiming is a part of the hazard of life. Just as being born is an ordeal, so staying alive is one also. As it is

> Better to have loved and lost
> Than never to have loved at all,

so it is better to have lived and been sick or even maimed than never to have lived at all. Never was the latter more dramatically proved than in the case of Franklin Delano Roosevelt. We must take our chances with disease and crippling accident; and, incidentally, God has nothing to do with either, save as sickness and maiming are challenges to us to conquer both. Recognizing the hazards of life does not make us fatalistic. God's counsel to our first parents, "Replenish the earth, *and subdue it*," is applicable to every scientific conquest of disease.

As our Lord spoke in the synagogue, he noticed her condition. It may be that he called her to him to illustrate some point in his message. The whole service of worship was stopped while Jesus stooped to heal one to whom his heart went out in the deepest compassion. This may seem strange to us, with our careful orders of worship. However, Jewish worship, although formal in places and always completely reverent, on occasion gave opportunity for a normal and natural interplay between the worshipers and the one who was leading the service. This part of the service is much like a modern informal midweek prayer and testimony meeting in an evangelical church. If Jesus had been speaking on the power of God, the dramatic nature of the healing would clinch his message in the minds of people as nothing else could. The woman, after her cure, gave God the praise in a testimony of passion and power.

In another place I will discuss the matter of the Sabbath healings of our Lord. Any place—and at any time—was a place of healing and service in the thinking of Jesus.[6] On every occasion we find Jesus standing against a narrow legalism. It has been claimed that the analogy between an ox that needs daily watering and a woman who had suffered for eighteen years is not sound. The woman could easily have waited until the next day. But the whole point is that a woman is of much greater value than an ox. If she had suffered for eighteen years, all the more reason to give her relief today, not tomorrow. Luke's phrase is typical of the beauty of his writing, "Ought not this woman, being a *daughter of Abraham*, . . . be loosed?" Luke, a Gentile, catches the vital and high-minded patriotism of Jesus— the value of a person comes before the laws of a state, or even of a religion. Jesus went to the heart of the matter in his protest against a false religiosity, "Thou hypocrite." Devotion to the law here was a red herring to cover the bitter antipathy to Jesus himself. How often loyalty to the less keeps us from being true to the greater. For many of the contemporaries and opponents of Jesus the law had become a fetish, an idol, a minor god. They made it an effective barrier which shielded them from an honest confrontation with the Eternal and his righteous demands. "Thus have ye made the commandment of God of none effect by your tradition," Jesus keenly observed. For practical purposes God's will and way were ruled out of their universe. To-day many moderns accomplish the same result with more apparent logic and subtlety, but the end product is still the same. Science, education, and the pride of life are often the red herrings that keep us from facing Christ's claims honestly. T. S. Eliot knows this well:

[6] Klausner agrees with the contemporary critics of Jesus in saying that he erred in healing on the Sabbath (*Jesus of Nazareth*, pp. 278-79). See also Montefiore, *op. cit.*, II, 501.

O weariness of men who turn from GOD
To the grandeur of your mind and the glory of your action,
To arts and inventions and daring enterprises,
To schemes of human greatness thoroughly discredited. [7]

Montefiore suggests here the real argument of Jesus, though it is not expressed, is that healing is not work; deeds of compassion are not labor.[8] Not only did the woman give God the glory, but the multitude rejoiced as well.

## III. The Woman Who Touched the Hem of His Garment
### —Matt. 9:18-22; Mark 5:25-34; Luke 8:43-48

In some ways one of the most poignant of the records of the healings of Jesus is that in connection with the woman who touched the hem of his garment. Matthew, Mark, and Luke all record the story. Mark is fond of stories within stories. Here is one that is intimately bound up with the account of the healing of Jairus' daughter. Jesus was proceeding to the home of Jairus, walking through the narrow streets of the town, far narrower than we Westerners can imagine. In some places one can extend both hands and touch the opposite walls in an Oriental town. A great crowd was accompanying Jesus. In crowds the individual is lost. The personality is often merged with the collective personality that belongs to the group. Psychologists say that this crowd or mob personality is always on a lower level than the individual personality of its components. We know that this story underlines the fact that it was the individual in the crowd who was of concern to Jesus. The mass was nothing; the person in his need was everything.

A woman pushed through the throng, reached out her hand and, with a feeling of magic mingled with hope, touched the hem of his garment. There was the inevitable amount of jostling and pushing you could expect in such narrow quarters. Great though the need of many individuals in the crowd may be, the

[7] From *The Rock*. Used by permission of Harcourt, Brace & Co., publisher.
[8] *Op. cit.*, II, 501.

resources in the person of Jesus are there only for those who make the claim of faith. Suddenly our Lord stopped and asked the arresting question, "Who touched me?" Mark tells us that Jesus immediately realized that power had gone out of him. The woman too was conscious of this exchange of healing virtue. It was the faith of the woman that was involved in her healing, as Jesus later pointed out, but it was faith to touch one who had demonstrated by his every action that he had a surplus of spiritual energy as seen by his concern for all in need—at this very moment he was on a mission of mercy—and his deep love for a despairing humanity.

> What of that other energy whose force
> Is not confined within a bomb; whose course,
> Undeviating, could obliterate
> From all the earth duplicity and hate
> If but released? How, once, the Master strove
> To teach all men alike the power of Love! [9]

In response to the demanding inquiry of Jesus a timid little woman finally came forward. Her malady was such that she instinctively had hidden it from others. Mark with sardonic bluntness says that for twelve years she had spent everything on doctors and "had suffered many things of many physicians." When Luke came to the story, he toned down immeasurably the criticism of his own profession by saying that she was a chronic case, who could not "be healed of any." He implied that the condition was hopeless from a medical standpoint. This woman was deprived of the consolation of worship, because her illness made her ceremonially unclean. Somehow, when the sufferer learned that Jesus was passing in the crowd, she felt that if she could just reach out and touch the tassel (*zizith*) of his garment, she would be made whole. The robe called the tallith was a sacred symbolical garment worn by every adult male

[9] Mary F. Legler, "Old Power for New," *Christian Century*, Sept. 10, 1947. Used by permission.

Jew. Its tassels were of white and blue wool. They were a token of consecration to the God of Israel (Num. 15:38-40) and were not considered to have any healing value. It was the person who wore the garment who made the difference.

Had He not wrought wondrous cures? He was the friend of the sinful and the unclean; He would not despise her. She would go to Him even in the crowd. Think of the courage needed for that venture—she unclean, to enter the crowd, to run the risk of exposure, shame, punishment! But her faith was strong with the urgency of her need. She dared not speak to Him—that would call attention of the multitude to an unclean person in their midst. But she said to herself, "If I touch but His garments I shall be made whole." She crept silently through the crowd behind Him, and touched the fringe of His cloak. At once the thrill of health—of freedom from her weary prison—passed through her. "She felt in her body that she was healed of her plague." It was the touch of faith; and it liberated for her the resources of divine compassion and power. [10]

Jesus knew, despite all the jostling, that spiritual energy had gone out of him. The disciples considered his question, "Who touched me?" absurd, but the woman did not, nor did Jesus, for he was keenly sensitive to his enviroment. There was a certain element of magic that entered into the action of the woman. To her, Jesus was a great rabbi and healer; possibly there would be healing value in his very garment. Later in the history of Christianity it was said that even the shadow of Peter brought help to those who were ill. Jesus wanted to raise her faith from the area that bordered on magic to a personal experience. That is why he did not hesitate to call out and ask who had touched him, even though it meant embarrassment to the person involved. Jesus was never satisfied to leave one physically better and not spiritually renewed.

After she told her story, with the utmost compassion Jesus said, "Daughter, thy faith hath made thee whole; go in peace." With what infinite tenderness he used the word "daughter." It

[10] Lang, *op. cit.*, p. 84.

is the only place the word employed in addressing a person is found in the New Testament, and it appears but a few times in the book of Ruth. The touch of faith had brought relief—evident and immediate. Healing did not come until it was summoned by the stretched-forth hand. "The energy of faith reached and drew forth the answering energy of grace." [11] The secret needs of a solitary life drew upon the infinite power and compassion that were in Jesus. Only when the one with need had faith to claim the divine resource was there the transference of the liberating and healing power available to any who would reach forth.

There are some interesting conjectures the story brings forth. If the woman had hurried away without acknowledging what she had done, there would still have been physical recovery, but she would have left with a greater faith in the garment than in the Man. Jesus was concerned that her faith be morally effective, as well as physically helpful. In the healing the Master made plain that it was not the touch, nor was it even "my power," but it was her faith that had made her whole.

So Jesus was graciously at work healing, teaching, inspiring, because he had learned the greatest of all lessons—that we rise through service. Women by their very nature as mothers and homemakers demonstrate this to us. The poet caught this mood in the conclusion of her poem about pots and pans:

> Although I must have Martha hands, I have a Mary mind;
> And when I black the boots, I try, Thy sandals, Lord, to find.

Brother Lawrence had discovered this truth long before her day. Browning may have put it with more artistry, but certainly not with more effectiveness, in two famous passages:

> I never realized God's birth before—
> How he grew likest God in being born.

> Such ever was love's way—to rise, it stoops.

[11] *Ibid.*, p. 91.

# 10

## So Great Faith

F AITH, hope, love, these three," according to Paul, are virtues beyond compare. Again and again Jesus laid emphasis upon the mountain-moving power of faith. The New Testament usually exhorts the individual to greater faith, but occasionally faith operates in behalf of others. Those who have faith are able by their trust to bring a blessing to a friend in need. This is seen particularly in the account of the paralytic borne by four of his friends, and in the incident of the healing of the centurion's servant.

I. HEALING OF A PARALYTIC—*Mark 2:1-12; Matt. 9:1-8; Luke 5: 17-26*

Jesus had just completed an evangelistic tour throughout Galilee. On his return to Capernaum, his headquarters at this particular time, a large crowd gathered in the home in which he was residing. The house may have been that of Simon Peter. The record goes on to say that Jesus preached "the word" unto them. We can be certain that as he expounded the Scripture, giving the wisdom of God from the deep resources of his own supreme personality, it was a rich revelation. The people, fascinated by such truth, did not want to give way so much as an inch to allow space for a sick man carried in on a litter. Blessed words were falling from the lips of a teacher who not only challenged, but who made one strangely dissatisfied to continue to drift on the low planes of life. In the group were official investigators, possibly scribes sent on a special mission to check on the teaching of the new Galilean rabbi. Mark's comment—they were "sitting there"—gives evidence of an official or semiofficial group.

The four men, seeing the impossibility of reaching Jesus by ordinary means, carried their paralyzed friend up the outside stairs of the building onto the flat Oriental roof. They could look down through the usual opening by which light entered and sun-dried produce was lowered into the house, and both see and hear Jesus beneath. Why not enlarge this opening and lower their burden to the source of help? It was no sooner thought of than the ease with which it could be done was apparent, for there was little difficulty in removing a few tiles or turning back the baked clay roof covering.[1] The word translated in our common version "palsy"[2] literally means "weak-kneed" and is used rather freely of any disease which might prevent a man from walking. Whatever was his difficulty, the four bearers believed that Jesus could do something about it. They were willing to go to the difficulty of breaking up a roof and disturbing the meeting below in order to bring the sick man to the attention of Jesus.

The dramatic quality that enters into any situation when a public meeting is disturbed was indelibly impressed upon me as a young man. It was in the early days of the "roaring twenties" when the stage had become particularly brazen. My father, John Roach Straton, was scheduled to meet the theatrical producer, William A. Brady, in a debate on the low estate to which the stage had fallen. The time came for the debate, and Brady had not appeared. The master of ceremonies asked if Brady was in the audience. As there was no reply, he said that Dr. Straton

[1] C. C. Torrey, in his translation of the four Gospels, does not follow Wellhausen, who thinks that the words "they uncovered the roof" are a mistranslation of an Aramaic phrase meaning "they brought him to the roof." Wellhausen's view is that Jesus was teaching on the flat roof. See Torrey, *The Four Gospels*.

[2] παραλυτικός.

would go ahead with his presentation. Just then Brady, with all of the flair for dramatically-timed entrances for which he was famous, stepped out in the aisle and said, "William A. Brady is here!" The electric results upon the audience must have been similar for the incident we are considering.

It has always been true that one can find a way to Jesus when there is a real desire. The record continues, "Jesus seeing their faith . . . " It was the faith of the four men who were willing to take extreme measures, and yet it was also the faith of the poor fellow who had such need, for the dramatic urgency of the whole incident leads us to believe that there had been other and unsuccessful attempts to introduce the sufferer to the great healer.

There is a social quality about faith. It cannot be learned; but, like bravery, it can be caught as it is imparted to those about one. Rudyard Kipling knew this when he wrote:

> If I were hanged on the highest hill,
>   *Mother o' mine, O mother o' mine!*
> I know whose love would follow me still,
>   *Mother o' mine, O mother o' mine!* [3]

A mother's faith and a mother's prayer have lifted many a man's life out of the miry clay and established his going.

One of the most vivid scenes in the Old Testament is the account of a band of ex-slaves who had fled Egypt. Pharaoh gave chase with a strong and well-equipped army. Before the Israelites was a vast water barrier, and behind them an avenging army. In terror the people cried out against Moses, "Why did you bring us out of Egypt?" Between them and mass panic stood the faith of one man, whose confidence in Jehovah soon became contagious: "Fear ye not, stand still, and see the salvation of the Lord." No wonder the author of Hebrews later could write of

[3] "Mother o' Mine" from *The Light That Failed*. Used by permission of Mrs. George Bambridge, Doubleday & Co., New York, and Macmillan & Co., London.

the incident, "By faith Moses" led the children of Israel as "they passed through the Red sea as by dry land."

Faith is not as the small boy defined it, "Believing something you know ain't so." It is trusting God to turn the present situation, no matter how dark, to the working out of his own divine purposes. The people caught the mood. They "glorified God, saying, We never saw it on this fashion."

Not only did Jesus observe the faith of the four bearers, but he likewise read the very heart of the sick man and saw that he could never be healed until he had a sense of forgiveness. A Jewish saying has it, "No sick man is healed until his sins have been forgiven him." [4] There was a wisdom about this great Galilean which has caused even modern psychiatrists to marvel. In the light of today's medical knowledge we see that possibly the man had a psychosis which caused the paralysis. It was as deep-seated as with Macbeth, who came to the doctor and inquired:

> Canst thou not minister to a mind diseased,
>
> . . . . . . . . . . . . . . . .
> And with some sweet oblivious antidote
> Cleanse the stuff'd bosom of that perilous stuff
> Which weighs upon the heart?

Jesus was aware of his need and so with deep concern said, "Son, thy sins be forgiven thee." It was a startling statement to all but the man involved. "So the sick man in the presence of the Holy One felt the yet unhealed wound of the soul, the aching of unforgiven sin." [5] As in Wagner's drama the unveiling of the Holy Grail caused the wound of Amfortas to quiver anew with pain, so it proved here. This announcement of forgiveness was a looming obstacle to the critical scribes of that time, and the consequent healing has been a stumbling block since to those

[4] Nedarim 41a. See also Montefiore, *op. cit.*, I, 43, in which he says that suffering or disease to the rabbis always implied sin.

[5] Lang, *op. cit.*, p. 66.

who would doubt the power of God. Yet the difficulty is not as large today as a generation ago, for modern psychiatry teaches that an illness or a paralysis can definitely be traced to a sense of sin. The psychiatrist calls it a "guilt reaction" and recognizes that the one who can give the most help in such a situation is a minister or a priest who will assure the patient of God's forgiveness. G. K. Chesterton, when asked why he joined the church, replied, with a great deal more wisdom than some moderns realize, "To get rid of my sins." In one of his famous detective stories Father Brown, who captures criminals by trying to reconstruct their thinking, says:

No man is really any good until he knows how bad he is, or might be; till he has realized exactly how much right he has to all this snobbery and sneering and talking about "criminals" as if they were apes in a forest ten thousand miles away; till he's got rid of all the dirty self-deception of talking about low types and deficient skulls; till he's squeezed out of his soul the last drop of the oil of the Pharisees; till his only hope is somehow or other to have captured one criminal, and kept him safe and sane under his hat. [6]

The blessed sense of sin's forgiveness is still a powerful motivating factor in a genuine religious faith.

It is well to recognize that we come here to a difficult gospel passage that has caused endless debate. The title "Son of man" in an apparent messianic sense is used prior to the great confession of Peter at Caesarea-Philippi. There is a definite claim of forgiveness of sin which is supported by a miracle. Some scholars hold that the incident about forgiveness of sins is a later insertion. If this is so, why all the doctrinal discussion, and why was not some other healing, such as the cleansing of a leper, chosen to convey the teaching, for leprosy was believed to be a definite proof of sin? Let us put aside for a moment further answer to the above problems. It is certainly true that when Mark was written, Jesus was considered to be the divine "Son of man,"

[6] Quoted in *Christendom*, Autumn, 1945, p. 484.

who had the power to forgive sins. For early New Testament Christians, as for us, the authority of Jesus in the field of religion starts with the forgiveness of sins.

In announcing the forgiveness of sin, Jesus recognized as well as the investigating committee that God alone would have this power, but here was human need, and our Lord never turned men away. Let them make the most of his statement. For himself the inference is plain, and his enemies got it. A priest or a prophet could pronounce divine forgiveness. Nathan did so in the case of David's ugly sin (II Sam. 12:13). "Forgiveness to a Jew of the age of Jesus, and even to Jesus himself, had a human and a divine side," as Montefiore points out.[7] The scribal reaction was due mainly to the antipathy which they bore Jesus. They were looking for a *cause célèbre*, and quite naturally here was a good one. A theory about sin being connected with disease did not cause them to question other healings of our Lord. Their reaction was that it was arrogant presumption on the part of Jesus. "Who can forgive sins but only God?" Jesus would have agreed with them. But if a priest or prophet had the right to *pronounce divine forgiveness*, certainly the Messiah had that same prerogative. For Jesus, the situation involved a quibble. His actions were always the same when confronted with a similar situation. Witness his reaction to Sabbath breaking. Jesus was much more of a prophet than he was a teacher or healer. His mind and those of his interrogators ran in different channels. Here was an immediate opportunity to show the power of God. The poor fellow needed help; help could come only by persuading him that he possessed divine forgiveness. From the close knowledge that Jesus had of his heavenly Father he was willing to assert the forgiveness of sin on the authority of his own person. He did not propose to let a theological question interfere with his ministry, for he knew that not until the cause was removed

---

[7] *Op. cit.,* I, 49.

could the effect be removed.[8] John Macmurray with modern wisdom has written:

> The purpose of the forgiveness of sins as a principle of life is the continual removal of fear and the isolation that springs from fear. The sense of guilt isolates a man from his fellows, because it carries with it the feeling that his fellows have a right to punish him. The forgiveness of sin therefore expresses a social attitude which restores self-confidence and maintains a consciousness which overcomes any sense of isolation.[9]

The reaction was immediate and electric. Not only did Jesus read the mind of the paralyzed man, but he could see the black thoughts in the hearts of the investigators: "Why doth this man thus speak blasphemies? who can forgive sins but God only?" In their small souls the gracious assurance of healing and forgiveness was forgotten in a theological dispute. It is well to be loyal to the truth, but it is tragic when what we consider to be loyalty keeps us from accepting the mercy and forgiveness a good God would surely bestow.

Bruce has remarked, "What Jesus had said did not necessarily amount to more than a declaration that there was no reason for despair in past sins." [10] It was not a technical absolution, "I absolve thee," but it was a declaration of divine forgiveness in this case. However, the whole account, and especially the reaction of the crowd, gives evidence that more than this was involved.

Jesus went on to take the opportunity afforded by the censure of the investigators to claim the messianic right of pronouncing forgiveness: "That ye may know that the Son of man hath power on earth to forgive sins (he saith to the sick of the

[8] As against Bultmann, Klostermann, and others who hold that it is a doctrinal accretion to the original story, William Manson says, "We must see in the forgiveness-declaration of Jesus the core of the original narrative" (*The Gospel of Luke*, p. 53).

[9] *Creative Society*, p. 100.

[10] *Op. cit.*, p. 167.

palsy,) I say unto thee, Arise, and take up thy bed, and go thy way into thine house. And immediately he rose, took up the bed, and went forth." Although "Son of man" in some instances means simply "man," in Daniel and in the Similitudes of Enoch it is definitely messianic. The difficult question about how "Son of man" is used here cannot be treated in full. It could have meant simply "I" in the Aramaic Jesus was speaking, yet by the time Mark was written it would have possessed its full messianic meaning. Devout and able scholars are divided on this point, largely because of its use here apparently before the messianic disclosure at Caesarea-Philippi. Yet there is no reason why in the heat of the controversy Jesus might not have employed it with its definite messianic meaning. The context of the story seems to indicate that he did use it with this meaning. Questions were already being raised about who this rabbi was and what was his authority; that is why the official investigators were present. As Jesus said *"bar-nasha"* in Aramaic, he could well have meant "Son of man" in its apocalyptic sense or simply "I." The interpretation would depend on the bias of the hearers. It fitted their purpose to say, "This man blasphemeth." To Jesus as the "Son of man" blasphemy was no more evident than it would have been for a prophet to have pronounced divine forgiveness.

The consciousness of forgiveness was immediate. As the paralytic had searched his own heart and as it leaped forth in penitence to accept the divine forgiveness, he heard the words, "Take up thy bed, and go thy way." Some would say that Jesus is simply employing the power of suggestion. There is unquestionably power in suggestion, but we are dealing with a far larger source of energy here, for there is the godly life plus definite faith in the power of God to heal. B. W. Bacon has reminded us of the close connection between healing and the forgiveness of sin. It was "inseparable in the teaching both of the synagogue and of the early church." [11] We think at once of Ps. 103:3, "Who forgiveth all thine iniquities; who healeth all thy diseases." Adolph Harnack, in a very beautiful passage, pointed out that the ancient world found the gospel of the healing Christ one that was peculiarly attractive, for the pagan gods were interested in only the healthy and the strong. He says that it is significant that it was Asclepius, the god of healing, who held out longest against Christianity. Harnack's words are:

Jesus says very little about sickness; he cures it. He does not explain that sickness is health; he calls it by its proper name, and is sorry for the sick person. There is nothing sentimental or subtle about Jesus; he draws no fine distinctions, and utters no sophistries about healthy people being really sick and sick people really healthy. . . . Jesus does not distinguish rigidly between sicknesses of the body and of the soul; he takes them both as different expressions of one supreme ailment in humanity.[12]

Celsus, with scorn, said that Christianity attracts only the sick, sinful, and foolish people. "He had not realized that what the ordinary man needs is not an *explanation* of evil, but the defeat of evil." [13]

## II. HEALING OF THE CENTURION'S SERVANT—*Matt. 8:5-13; Luke 7:1-10*

The once-paralyzed man had received forgiveness and healing because both he and his friends had possessed faith to persevere in the face of great obstacles. In the story of the healing of the centurion's servant we see such faith that even Jesus marveled. Both evangelists are evidently using the same account, which originally was found in Q, the document composed of common material in Matthew and Luke that is not found in Mark. It is unique because it is one of possibly two narratives in

[11] *Studies in Matthew*, p. 391.
[12] *Expansion of Christianity*, I, 101.
[13] Richardson, *op. cit.*, p. 68.

Q—the other in Luke 11:14; Matt. 12:22-30. In both Gospels
it follows the great sermon by Jesus, and the location is Capernaum. We observe that Gentiles were involved in the only two
instances of healing at a distance. The other case was that of the
daughter of the Syrophoenician woman. Concerning the possibility of such remote healings Rudolph Otto, after carefully
discussing them in the light of modern psychical research, comes
to this conclusion:

> The sceptic's comment is: Surely no one believes in an operation at
> a distance like this. We reply: Quite so, if it were not better instead
> of passing facile judgment to study for once the matter itself and
> its actual setting, i.e., in actual and attested experience. . . . How the
> phenomena may be explained is another matter, but that they occur
> as actual phenomena is today no longer in question. [14]

These incidents were peculiarly appealing to the Early Church
because of the Gentiles who were in that church. When they
were sick, even though Jesus was not present, they believed that
healing would come through faith in him. The centurion, then,
becomes a type of the believing Gentile.

Luke begins this story at an earlier point in the narrative than
does Matthew. He says that emissaries were first sent to ask
healing for the slave who was seriously ill. Although there are
differences in the narrative portion of the two records, the
dialogue is practically the same. There are similarities in this
account and the record of the healing of the nobleman's son and
the Syrophoenician woman's daughter, but the differences
between this account and that of the nobleman's son are quite
marked.

The remarkable feature of this story is far more the faith of
the centurion than the miracle of healing which accompanied
the faith. This Roman officer was a "God-fearer" who had built
a synagogue for the Jewish people. At modern Tel Hum, the ancient site of Capernaum, the ruins of a synagogue of rare beauty

[14] *Op. cit.*, p. 349.

PREACHING THE MIRACLES OF JESUS

have been unearthed. Some have thought that the exquisite mosaics in its floor were the very ones across which the feet of our Lord passed. However, it is probably to be dated around A.D. 200, for the earlier Jewish synagogues were apparently destroyed by Titus or Hadrian. It is quite possible that the ruins we can see today are built on the site of an older Jewish place of worship, and, "therefore, it may safely be regarded as a reconstruction of the one in which Jesus himself taught." [15]

Certainly this foreign centurion was a man of great faith. Is it strange that Jesus "marvelled"? The servant back home lay "sick of the palsy." It is the same technical word for paralysis which is used in the above account, and yet the sick man may have been suffering from a different malady. The centurion believed with such fervor in the power of the great teacher and healer of Galilee that he felt that Jesus had only to say the word and his servant would be healed. This officer was a remarkable man. Notice his genuine humility, his great faith, and his humanity toward a sick slave, which was unusual for the ancient world. He exhibited the essence of courtesy in recognizing that Jesus, as a strict Jew, would be subject to ceremonial defilement if he came into the household of a pagan. "Lord, I am not worthy that thou shouldest come under my roof." He believed that there was power in Jesus because of his innate authority, and that the "boy" would be healed. "But speak the word only, and my servant shall be healed. For I am a man under authority having soldiers under me: and I say to this man, Go, and he goeth; and to another, Come, and he cometh; and to my servant, Do this, and he doeth it."

Jesus marveled at the man. In the centurion there is a remarkable fusion of qualities that make for greatness in any field. He was a soldier of some prominence, or he would not have held the position he did. As such, his courage was obvious to all. He was every inch the Roman, yet he had discovered the blessed

[15] Jack Finegan, *Light from the Ancient Past*, p. 228. See also discussion in this volume, p. 192.

faculty of living in peace with his neighbors. Many of the ancients were attracted by the high monotheism and the ethical demands of the Hebrew religion. It was far and away the best of its day. The manly soldier was among this number. He possessed a frank humility that is rare indeed. With a simplicity born of both strength and humility he asked for help for one he loved. His own authority in the field of command led him to believe that Jesus exerted like authority in the field of faith.

The centurion came "beseeching him" for his slave. As a man of authority he expected obedience and respect from this very servant, but notice how he blends affection with his authority. After all, it is the union of these two qualities that brings efficiency and accomplishment. As he expected both respect and obedience, so he exhibited them in the presence of our Lord. No wonder Jesus could say that he had not found a like quality or a like faith, no, not in Israel. Building upon it Jesus said with assurance, "Go thy way; and as thou hast believed, so be it done unto thee. The centurion's faith in the authority of Jesus was justified, for the record concludes, "And his servant was healed in the selfsame hour." This Gentile God-fearer knew that Jesus had authority in the only realm that ultimately matters, the realm of the spirit. He did, and the servant was healed. Man is a spirit like the God who made him and breathed into his body the breath of life. When men forget or when an age forgets it, tragedy always ensues. A scintillating modern poet sees it:

> And man is a spirit
>   And symbols are his meat,
> So pull not down the steeple
>   In your monied street.
>
> For money chimes feebly,
>   Matter dare not sing—
> Man is a spirit,
>   Let the bells ring. [16]

[16] "Holes in the Sky." Copyright 1948 by Louis MacNeice. Reprinted by permission of Random House, Inc.

Faith in the power of God's Son has always worked wonders. It is one of the most important things in the world. In our own day Albert Schweitzer has taught us of its power, and also of the graciousness of the healing ministry in the name of Christ. One of the most outstanding incidents in the whole educational world in recent years was the tercentenary of Harvard University. On this gala occasion that great school of learning conferred degrees upon outstanding men in the realms of science, literature, and the arts. They brought in leaders in various fields from all over the world for this purpose. Wishing to do honor to Albert Schweitzer, New Testament scholar supreme, musical genius extraordinary, philosopher profound, the committee sent to the Belgian Congo and asked that he come to Harvard University to receive a degree on this notable occasion. Schweitzer wrote back that he appreciated greatly the consideration and the honor, but that he was too busy caring for the sick natives in the name of Jesus to come to Cambridge to receive the degree. He went undecorated by the university, but he had long before learned that faith in Jesus and devotion to the art and skill of healing in his name were far better gifts. Is it little wonder that men of superb intellect themselves have acclaimed the doctor from Lambaréné as the greatest living man?

# 11

## Sabbath Made for Man

JESUS' attitude toward the Sabbath was a very large factor in his clash with the religious authorities which culminated in his death. Altogether there are seven records of cures on the Sabbath.[1] In most of the cases a controversy developed because of the healing. At first glance those Sabbath controversies seem to be religious squabbles which do not strike fire for us today, but on closer investigation we see that Jesus was contending for a very vital principle. Instead of being secondary, the whole matter is of the utmost importance, for the Sabbath healings demonstrate conclusively the instinctive humanitarianism of our Lord. It was in the very essence of his being to champion men in their every need. God had placed the earth and its fullness at man's disposal. Institutions, no less than other resources, were not ends in themselves but were for the benefit of mankind. "The sabbath was made for man, and not man for the sabbath." Jesus supported the temple and delighted to be within its portals, just as he supported by his regular attendance and participation worship on the Sabbath day. But as did the prophets of Israel, Jesus saw that even the most sacred of institutions would pass away if the life of the spirit was being hindered thereby. His

---

[1] Healing of the man with the withered hand (Mark 3:1-5); exorcising the demon in the Capernaum synagogue (Mark 1:21-28); healing Peter's mother-in-law (Mark 1:29-31); the hunchbacked woman (Luke 13:10-17); the man with dropsy (Luke 14:1-6); the invalid man at the pool of Bethesda (John 5:1-15); the man born blind (John 9:1-7). The first three are treated in this chapter along with the Sabbath question. The others are found under different headings.

127

concern was to do everything possible to preserve this spirit.

Jesus said, "I am come that they might have life, and that they might have it more abundantly." His Sabbath healings were evidence that he meant business, for under the Jewish law Sabbath breaking was a capital offense. There was a valid reason for this Sabbath strictness. It had become one of the major instruments for cultural survival, as Elton Trueblood points out:

When Jerusalem fell, in 586 B.C., and the leaders, their temple having been wantonly destroyed, were taken to Babylon in captivity, their chance of survival was slight. The northern kingdom had fallen more than a hundred years earlier and had never been revived. It has not been revived to this day. The southern kingdom would have gone the same way, and the whole of Western civilization would have been greatly impoverished thereby, if the prophet Ezekiel and others like him had not placed great emphasis on the Sabbath. The Sabbath observance became an external badge which held the people together as by a public witness. [2]

On the Sabbath you could walk a little over half a mile—the Sabbath day's journey referred to in the Scripture—but no more. You could heal a dangerously sick person, but not a chronically-ill one. You could take the ox out of the ditch, because its valuable life was in danger, as Jesus succinctly pointed out. Our Lord rebelled against the injustice which would permit a poor woman to continue to be bent double, though she had suffered already for eighteen years, and so he healed her, Sabbath or no Sabbath. Yet Jesus would have been the last one to have been interested in breaking down the religious observance of God's day, for we find him always in his place in the synagogue, "as was his custom"; he added to the understanding of the day that it was man's as well as God's. Jesus would have had no patience with Emily Dickinson's revolt against the Sabbath:

> Some keep the Sabbath going to church;
> I keep it staying at home,

[2] *Foundations for Reconstruction,* p. 42.

With a bobolink for a chorister,
  And an orchard for a dome.

. . . . . . . . . . . . .

God preaches,—a noted clergyman,—
  And the sermon is never long;
So instead of getting to heaven at last,
  I'm going all along! [3]

He knew well the value of corporate worship. He was faithful to God's house on God's day. Yet he added to the understanding of the day that it was man's as well as God's.

Without going into the question of religious forms and institutions in general we can agree that forms and regulation in the Hebrew-Christian tradition served definite moral ends. We have just noticed the value of Sabbath observance in giving a sense of cohesion that did much to preserve Jewish ethical monotheism. Where the forms lapse, it is difficult to maintain the content the forms carry. Church and synagogue attendance is a case in point. Outward conformity may not mean inner power; but certainly religious power is difficult, if not impossible, to keep apart from the observances that go with it. The whole sacramental view of life and religion comes in here. Jesus, by his actions as well as his words, was in the prophetic tradition when he contended for forms and institutions more suited to advancing inner states. "These ought ye to have done, and not to leave the other undone." It is possible that our Lord thought of the banding together of his followers which was to develop into "my church" as a continuation of the Old Testament "remnant" concept.

## I. THE MAN WITH THE WITHERED HAND—*Mark 2:23-3:6; Matt. 12:1-14; Luke 6:1-11*

In the account of the healing of the man with the withered hand we have the whole matter of the Sabbath controversy

---

[3] From *The Poems of Emily Dickinson*, edited by Martha Dickinson Bianchi and Alfred Leete Hampson. Used by permission Little, Brown & Co.

brought to a sharp focus. The Sabbath was the great Jewish religious institution. By its absolute prohibition of labor it dramatically and regularly reminded men of both the supremacy of God and his concern for the well-being of men and animals that a recurring period of rest provided. Jesus believed profoundly that it was for man's benefit. Yet when its meticulous observances infringed on fundamental human rights, Jesus ignored the regulations. The matter came to a head one day when the disciples plucked and ate some grains of wheat by the roadside as they journeyed. Notice that it is often the disciples, rather than Jesus himself, who occasion controversy, though Jesus defends their actions. As a whole the disciples were in the category of 'am hā 'āretz. The phrase translated "men of the land" is best rendered by our term "the common people." It was a term sometimes used in derision and often, though not always, had a particular reference to people living in Galilee. They were not too careful about the minutiae of the law. These "common people" instinctively realized that such petty rules were of little real importance. Because the disciples pulled the grain, they were reaping. When they rubbed it between their hands to remove the chaff, they were threshing. On both counts this was reckoned as work which was forbidden. There is no problem about plucking the grain, for legally anyone who had need could help himself in order to allay his hunger. According to this enlightened and beneficent Jewish regulation, no one had the right to keep a hungry man from the bounty provided by God's earth.

Meticulous Sabbath observance became a touchstone of narrow orthodoxy. As interpreted by the Pharisees it ministered to their own spiritual pride rather than set forth the greatness of God. So they watched with eagle eye for some breach of the regulations which would permit them to bring an accusation against Jesus. They asked him, "Why do they do on the sabbath day that which is not lawful?" Observe the defense of Jesus. It was biblical, for one thing. He pointed out the precedent

David had set (I Sam. 21:1-6) when Ahimelech—Mark's text wrongly has Abiathar—permitted David and his warriors to eat the consecrated bread. Jesus used this story of David's exploits because it came closer to illustrating his position than any other. There was certainly the difference that David and his men were in desperate need of food, while this could hardly be said of the disciples. The point at issue, which was true both of David and of the disciples of Jesus, is that human requirements and benefits always take precedence over any legal regulation. It has been pointed out by Jewish scholars that the position of Jesus regarding the Sabbath was essentially that of modern liberal Judaism. Men are always of greater value than laws, so Jesus went on to say, "The sabbath was made for man, and not man for the sabbath."

Mark, for convenience in his discussion of the attitude of Jesus toward the Sabbath, ties up the above incident with the healing which immediately follows in the text. However, the two incidents are related in subject matter rather than in time, for Mark is here following a topical rather than a chronological sequence. If this was not the case, we would have to hold that our Lord and his disciples were going through the fields on their way to the synagogue when, to assuage their hunger, they plucked, rubbed, and ate the raw grain on the way. Such a situation is highly unlikely; it is much more probable that a period of time separated the events.

On the Sabbath day on which the second account took place the accusers of Jesus had spotted in the congregation a man with a withered hand. When Jesus entered, they carefully watched to see what would take place, for they had rightly guessed what his reaction would be. His enemies thereby gave him the sincerest flattery. This was not the only incident in which they judged correctly that his action would be one of mercy, of kindness, of forgiveness. An interesting side light is the fact that they took for granted the healing power of Jesus.

In every case Jesus rose to such a challenge. It takes courage

131

of the highest character never to back away from a sharp issue because of expediency. In the Levitical law violation of the Sabbath was punishable by death (Exod. 31:14; 35:2). Healing was classified as work and therefore prohibited unless the case was so serious that life would otherwise be forfeited. Later the Mishna said that those who defile the Sabbath are cut off from heaven—which would correspond to excommunication (Sanhedrin 7:8).

Jesus commanded the unfortunate fellow to stand up. Turning to the group, whose questions he read plainly in their minds, he said unto them, "Is it lawful to do good on the sabbath days, or to do evil? to save life, or to kill?" The position of Jesus was that no healing or good action should be postponed because of the Sabbath. The heart immediately gives an affirmative answer, but here men were stiffened by a narrow legalism, so they kept quiet.

The record goes on, "And when he had looked round about on them with anger, being grieved at the hardness of their hearts . . ." Jesus knew the meaning of righteous wrath. Hard hearts ought always to make good men angry. Jesus was only intolerant when dealing with intolerance. Modern men of good will must learn what many of the Old Testament writers knew, and that is how to hate wickedness. Vice is all too often first endured, then pitied, then embraced rather than hated from the first.

Jesus said, "Stretch forth thy hand." The afflicted man had seen what had taken place. He had heard the question of Jesus, with its implication that God wills the good for men. Law is to save life, not constrict it. Here was a new prophet with a new point of view. Did the unfortunate one think, "Perhaps I can command these long-disused muscles"? The impulse to obey became overpowering when this rabbi spoke with a tone of helpful authority and commanded him to stretch forth his hand. He believed that it was possible, and so it proved. Jesus never asked for impossiblities. He knew God's power, and he knew that

God had limited himself by his own laws. He never asked his heavenly Father to grow a hand where one had been lost. The confidence that our Lord possessed was imparted to the man, and so healing came.

Jesus did not make a breach with the law, but with a narrow interpretation of the law. He backed his position with Scripture, plus an appeal to the oral law, which permitted an ox that had fallen into a ditch to be rescued.[4] Despite the result of the miracle the adversaries continued to plot how they might destroy Jesus. They had seen the healing with their own eyes; they had heard the words. The question of Jesus had searched their souls: "Is it lawful to do good on the sabbath days, or to do evil?" Had the fellow not been cured, they would have had no case against the Nazarene, but still their hearts were hard. Evidently the Pharisees preferred on the Sabbath to do evil—to plot the downfall of a good man rather than to give up their minute and meaningless regulations. The solution for legalism as held by this group of Pharisees was a return to the first principle of religion— that good might come to the sons of men. The supreme tragedy occurs when religion is employed to constrict and narrow life rather than to broaden it. God is good as well as great; and when we build on his goodness, we build on eternity. Sidney Lanier knew this:

> As the marsh-hen secretly builds on the watery sod,
> Behold I will build me a nest on the greatness of God:
> I will fly in the greatness of God as the marsh-hen flies.

## II. The Man with Dropsy—*Luke 14:1-6*

The question is again dealt with in the incident of healing the man with dropsy. There are parallels in this incident with the account of the healing of the woman with an issue of blood and the man with the withered hand. Matthew, in his account of the withered hand incident, even incorporates the argument of res-

---

[4] According to Matthew's account.

cuing an animal. Jesus may well have used this as an effective answer on more than one occasion.

Our Lord had been invited on the Sabbath day to a festive meal in the home of a Pharisee. He accepted the invitation in good faith. There are evidences that it was not so given, for the record—"they watched him"—indicates that the man with dropsy was brought in to make a test case. If there was a design on the part of the host, unquestionably the sick man was an innocent party to the whole procedure. Reviving the issue as stated in Luke 6:9, Jesus took the lead and asked the Pharisees, "Is it lawful to heal on the sabbath day?" Then without waiting for an answer, which they did not give anyway, he "healed him, and let him go." Jesus went on, "Which of you shall have an ass or an ox fallen into a pit, and will not straightway pull him out on the sabbath day?" There is a marginal reading that is adopted by Tischendorf along with Westcott and Hort which has "son" instead of "ass." The manuscript evidence is about equally divided between the two. As the Old Testament often couples the ox and the ass together, and as Jesus' speech was much colored by Old Testament thought, the latter word would come naturally to his lips. The contrast is evidently between the rescue of an animal and the healing of a man. This would not be the case if the reading "son" were adopted. Jesus by his question, which can have only one answer, again shows his recognition of the supreme value of human personality: "How much better is a man than an ox?"

III. The Man at the Pool of Bethesda—*John 5:1-16*

The controversy flared up again in connection with the healing of the man at the pool of Bethesda, or Bethzatha. The exact location of this particular spring is not known. Although excavations in this area have revealed a pool with five shallow arches on its north side, under the floor of an old crypt, there is no evidence that the five arches could be understood to be the "five porches." It may have been located in the newer northern section of Jerusalem, near the Sheep Gate. If so, this would give reason to believe that the correct reading is Bethzatha, which means "house of sheep." The whole matter of correct name and place is in a confused state due to variations in manuscripts, plus a lack of complete topographical knowledge of the Jerusalem of the first century. The "bubbling" of water would be satisfied by the Virgin's Well, Gihon, meaning "gusher." It was south of the temple area. The topographical references show that the author at least was evidently quite familiar with the location he was describing. The best manuscripts omit part of verse three and the whole of four, which refer to an angel moving the waters.

John tells us that this incident took place when there was a "feast of the Jews." This may have been a Passover, but there is no way of knowing. In any event, our Lord happened to be on the Sabbath day in the portico, where the pool was located. His heart was surely moved at all of the suffering which he saw there. Evidently picking out one particularly pitiful case, he asked the man, "Wilt thou be made whole?" The poor fellow in words of almost complete despair replied, "Sir, I have no man, when the water is troubled, to put me into the pool: but when I am coming, another steppeth down before me." Although the man had been sick for thirty-eight years, there is no indication that he had been at this particular pool for that length of time. Efforts to make the number thirty-eight of symbolic value are entirely too farfetched. His need was great, and it must have been discouraging indeed to be in such a state that others always secured the blessing before he could possibly get to the waters as they bubbled up.

Those who emphasize the symbolic in John see the "five porches" referring to the five books of Moses, which had failed to bring healing to the Jewish people. The "thirty-eight years" becomes a reference to the wandering of the Israelites in the wilderness, indicative of the confused state of the Jewish people that gave rise to the curative factor of the Christian faith. Before the symbolic interpretation is accepted as the best solution of this particular problem in John, the reader should weigh carefully the considered judgment of Bernard in connection with it. He points out that it would be much more natural for the author, if he were using symbolism primarily, to have "forty" rather than "thirty-eight." "While symbolic meaning may easily be read into the narrative once written, there is no probability that it was originally constructed in so artificial a fashion." [5]

From time immemorial certain bubbling springs have been thought to have curative values. That cures are wrought at Lourdes, in France, there is not the slightest doubt.[6] When people believe strongly enough that they will be healed if they can meet certain conditions, they often are made whole. The poor fellow in this account must have had both faith and patience to a remarkable degree. To see others go away evidently healed, to make the effort himself to reach the water and each time to be disappointed, shows a commendable persistence. He hoped against hope that the next time he might be able to make it. All of the above is prime psychological background for the cure. The response of Jesus to this situation was immediate, "Take up thy bed, and walk." The other sick about the pool had a chance, but not this man, and so Jesus provided the healing which the man wanted above all else in life.

Some scholars have seen in the story a parallel to Mark's healing of the paralytic (Mark 2:1-12). However, the setting is completely different. The onlookers are here not evidently impressed, and the crux of the Johannine story turns on the relation of Jesus to the Sabbath, while in Mark it is the forgiveness of sins. The almost verbal point in common of telling a man to take up his bed and walk would be expected when in both instances the sick men were lying on their pallets.

The fellow arose, took up his bed, and within a short time made for the temple to give God thanks for the healing brought to his body. Either on the way or right after he had arrived, still

[5] *Op. cit.*, I, 228-29.

[6] See the discussion in Alexis Carrel, *Man, the Unknown.*

carrying his bed mat, he was asked by the strict legalist of that day why he was carrying his bedding on the Sabbath. To do so was against the law. After recounting what had taken place, he went on, "He that made me whole, the same said unto me, Take up thy bed, and walk." When they asked where he was, he replied that he did not know.

The heart of the account is the Sabbath controversy and the appeal of the healed man to the authority of the one who had cured him and told him to take up his bed as sufficient reason for carrying the mat in violation of Sabbath regulations. Macgregor has well said, "The Christ who gives new life also has the power to free from the restraint of the old law." [7] This was evidently the first time that the Sabbath regulations had been broken in Jerusalem. Jesus was here facing the legalists in their home territory. In verse sixteen the imperfect tense in the Greek should be noted. It implies that Sabbath breaking was habitual with Jesus. "For this cause the Jews began to persecute Jesus, . . . because he began to do these things on the Sabbath." To this charge Jesus replied, "My Father worketh even until now, and I work." By such a statement Jesus at once passed onto much more dangerous ground. Sabbath breaking was bad enough, but for this Galilean to claim divine prerogatives was nothing short of blasphemy. The phraseology is the typical and mystical Johannine way of putting the synoptic expression, "The Son of man is Lord of the Sabbath." [8] John's major interest is, of course, the divine personality of Jesus, which is highlighted by the Sabbath question. Thus he dwells at length upon Jesus as the Son of God, which is implied by the claim to be Lord of the Sabbath.

The religion of formal enactment is confronted by the religion of spiritual freedom. The religion of the spirit challenges

[7] *Op. cit.*, p. 170.

[8] This is Bernard's position (*op. cit.*, I, 237). We cannot go here into the problem of what the phrase "Son of man" means in Mark 2:28. Most scholars hold, probably correctly, that in Mark it is simply the Aramaic way of saying, "Man is lord of the Sabbath." The evangelist could easily have had Mark's Greek text in mind as he wrote. See discussion on p. 118.

the religion of the letter. The universalism of the mind of Jesus is opposed by the particularism of those who stand by a specific code. To Jesus, sacred seasons and places were meant to be ministers to bless men, not chains to fetter men. All institutions are but means, not ends.[9]

The fat was in the fire in any event, for the narrow clique of legalists had determined on his life. Why should not Jesus then speak of the work that his Father was doing? "My Father is working still, and I am working." So they raged against him, because "he not only had broken the sabbath, but said also that God was his Father, making himself equal with God." What a unique filial consciousness this shows. Jesus knew himself to be the medium of the divine mind and the divine purpose, and did not hesitate to show this knowledge by his deeds and by his words. Do you remember Arthur Clough's "Bethesda"?

> I saw again the spirits on a day,
> Where on the earth in mournful case they lay;
> Five porches were there, and a pool and round,
> Huddling in blankets, strewn upon the ground,
> Tied-up and bandaged, weary, sore and spent,
> The maimed and halt, diseased and impotent.
> But what the waters of that pool might be,
> Of Lethe were they, or Philosophy;
> And whether he, long waiting, did attain
> Deliverance from the burden of his pain
> There with the rest; or whether, yet before
> Some more diviner stranger passed the door
> With his small company into that sad place,
> And breathing hope into the sick man's face,
> Bade him take up his bed, and rise and go.

Hope came to the hopeless because Jesus, the great humanitarian, healed on the Sabbath and on every other day. A need, not the day or occasion, called forth his mercy. "My Father worketh even until now, and I work."

[9] Major, Manson, and Wright, *op. cit.*, p. 757.

# 12

## Ears That Hear

A GREAT deal of sympathy has always been evoked for the blind, but, unfortunately, this has never been true of those who are afflicted with deafness. The deaf have been far more a subject for mirth than for pity; and yet, to the deaf, their affliction is certainly no laughing matter.

Dating from the time of Isaiah, one of the signs of the messianic age was to be the restoration of hearing to the deaf. "Then the eyes of the blind shall be opened, and the ears of the deaf shall be unstopped." (Isa. 35:5.) This passage unquestionably had an influence upon Jesus. In response to John's question, "Are you the Messiah?" Jesus said, "Shew John . . . the blind receive their sight, and the lame walk, the lepers are cleansed, *and the deaf hear*" (Matt. 11:5), a very evident reference back to the passage in Isaiah. Jesus is here putting himself in the very middle of the messianic stream. It is well to remember that the New Testament cannot be understood without reference to the Old. Our Old Testament was the only Bible Jesus and the first Christians possessed. They used it then in a very similar fashion to the way we employ today both the Old and the New Testaments. The tremendous influence exerted upon the New Testament by the Old is seen in Matthew's Gospel, where we find the author constantly looking for fulfillment of Old Testament passages. It is quite evident that the glad and joyous prophecies of Isaiah's kingdom age as well as other of the prophets had their specific impact upon the heart and mind of Jesus. Jesus quoted the scroll of Isaiah

(61:1-2) and said, "This day is this scripture fulfilled in your ears" (Luke 4:21).

It is difficult for us today fully to appreciate the messianic milieu or atmosphere of the first century. For the Jewish people, at least, it was the most dominant influence in their entire lives. They lived in an age that was looking for the Messiah. This is clearly seen in the two instances of Anna and Simeon in the temple when the baby Jesus was presented there according to the Jewish custom. Simeon exclaimed, "Mine eyes have seen thy salvation" (Luke 2:30). It was an age that expected certain things of the Messiah, such as the opening of blind eyes and the unstopping of deaf ears, along with other healing evidences. As we study the whole history of the world and of religious movements, we recognize that the Palestine of the first century furnished the only place and time when a Messiah could come and be recognized.

From the lips of the oppressed of that day was wrung the bitter cry, "How long, O Lord?" as each faithful Jew longed for the coming of the Messiah and the deliverance he would bring. At Caesarea-Philippi we hear the words of Peter, "Thou art the Messiah," and the joyous acknowledgment of Jesus, "Blessed art thou, Simon Bar-jona: for flesh and blood hath not revealed it unto thee, but my Father which is in heaven" (Matt. 16:17).[1] If the Nazarene was not the Messiah, the Old Testament prophecies and promise are all false, and there is no hope, for Jesus the Messiah came in the only age when a Messiah could come. The messianic milieu was never to be repeated. The glory that is Bach's music grew out of his age and his background. Were he writing today, he would write as the moderns, Shostakovich and the others. During the richness of the Elizabethan era the English language came to its flower, and Shakespeare was ready.

> The poem hangs on the berry bush
> When comes the poet's eye;

[1] There is not space here to discuss the critical questions involved.

The street begins to masquerade
When Shakespeare passes by. [2]

So in the fullness of time God sent forth his own Son, born of a woman, born under the law to redeem them that were under the law.

Men are a product of their age, and Jesus was no exception. He could do the work of his heavenly Father only as the Messiah, living, working, teaching, in the age in which he blessed the earth with his presence. Another day might not have harkened or understood, but first-century Palestine afforded the correct atmosphere. Before taking up specifically two instances of the healing of ears, we would do well to remember that Jesus himself taught that he came to open the ears of those spiritually deaf even more than to unstop the ears of those physically hard of hearing.

## I. THE DEAF MUTE—*Mark 7:31-37*

In Matt. 15:30 we have a catalogue of general instances of healing in which a multitude of the lame, blind, dumb, and maimed were restored by Jesus. Mark 7:31-37 gives one typical instance of healing. As nearly as we can tell it follows in point of time Jesus' return from the regions of Tyre. The locale was in the ten-city region, a non-Jewish area known as the Decapolis. There is some evidence from Mark's complicated geographical explanation which gives credence to the belief that Jesus was a refugee at the time and was skirting the territory of Herod Antipas.[3] According to Mark he would go north through Sidon, then turn east and finally south to the Decapolis. It is likely that the deaf man was a Greek. He could apparently speak with some difficulty, and this is an indication that he was not born deaf.

Friends who knew of the healing power of Jesus had brought

[2] William C. Gannett, "We See as We Are." Used by permission.

[3] So Major, Manson, and Wright, *op. cit.*, p. 103. Goguel likewise holds to this view (*op. cit.*, p. 367).

their afflicted companion to the Master. There is no suggestion of demon possession. Demons were cast out by a word. Here we have physical contact. Jesus varied his approach to correspond to the needs of the individual, so he took this man aside, recognizing, in all likelihood, the timidity of the patient. It was clear to Jesus that the crowd would have affected adversely the possibility of a cure. In sign language Jesus engaged in an interesting "conversation" with the deaf man. The fingers in the ears are symbolic of boring through the obstacle. The touching of the tongue would be of psychological advantage, for the man was well aware of his difficulty with speech. The looking up to heaven was an obvious way to say "God." Our present-day knowledge of hygiene, plus a Western sense of fitness, objects to the use of saliva as a curative agent. This, however, was a commonly accepted method in the days of Jesus and should cause us no undue concern. Its use occurs also in another Marcan healing, where the eyes of a blind man are opened (8:22-26). It is likewise employed in John (9:6). Tacitus tells us that the Emperor Vespasian cured a blind man in Alexandria in a somewhat similar fashion.[4] Then the deep sigh, which could be seen as well as heard by a normal person, would be indicative of earnestness and of possible prayer. So the great healer established rapport with the afflicted man by this evidence of sympathy and helpfulness, all of which was good psychology and definitely necessary to break down a psychic barrier. The whole account is strongly suggestive that a healing was about to take place. Finally Jesus, in his native language, said, "Ephphatha"—"that is, Be opened." The Aramaic word spoken to a Greek is a good indication of historic accuracy, because Jesus normally spoke Aramaic. If the Greek had possessed his hearing, Jesus would, in all likelihood, have spoken Greek.[5]

The crowd's reaction is of interest: "He hath done all things well: he maketh both the deaf to hear, and the dumb to speak."

[4] *History* IV. 81.
[5] So J. Newton Davies in the *Abingdon Bible Commentary*, p. 1009.

The last clause is evidently a reference to Isa. 35:5. The multitude would see in the situation a fulfillment of this passage. We have their own appraisal in the first part of the sentence. Those who saw at firsthand his ministry knew that he did all things well. From that day on his followers have known blessing in their lives when Jesus speaks. This is true whether he speaks through the gospel record of his ministry or through that closer fellowship that comes from intimate contact with the living Lord.

> Lord, speak to me, that I may speak
> In living echoes of Thy tone;
> As Thou hast sought, so let me seek
> Thine erring children lost and lone.

Is there any wonder that men have published to the four corners of the earth what faith in a mighty Christ has done for them?

The whole incident is of unusual interest because it shows Jesus as a physician operating as a healer of his day and yet adding to the physical means that divine power which, as the Messiah, he believed he possessed. Rudolph Otto has a very significant comment on this particular incident:

So it was with Christ's healing; it went beyond the exercise of mere skill in healing; he was a miraculous physician. But at the same time *he really was a physician,* and on occasion he used the remedies of folk medicine, anointing with oil. He healed . . . the man born blind, but he used the healing remedy, moistening the fingers with spittle; he did not accomplish the healing with one stroke, like the magicians, but as a healing process, gradually, and in stages.[6]

In our generation the healing ministry of Christ is multiplied a thousandfold. His words have come true, "Greater works than these shall he do; because I go unto my Father." Hospitals in every land bring hope and health in the name of Christ. They use the modern technique of scientific medicine to promote heal-

[6] *Op. cit.,* p. 356. Italics mine.

ing. These hospitals in our own and foreign lands would not be there at all were it not for consecrated surgeons, doctors, and nurses who staff them, and equally consecrated Christians who cannot themselves give the touch of healing but who show by their gifts that this work of Christ shall go on from strength to strength.

## II. THE EAR OF MALCHUS—*Luke 22:49-53; Matt. 26:51-53; Mark 14:47-48; John 18:10-11*

Mutilations or blemishes of any kind were especially abhorrent to the ancient Jew (Lev. 21:17-23). As Jesus was concerned that internal ears might hear properly, so the healing of the external ear of Malchus at the time of the arrest of our Lord can be adduced as evidence that outer disfigurement occasioned the same response of sympathy as did internal malady.

A well-organized and armed military force, guided by Judas, came to apprehend this disturbing Nazarene prophet. All four evangelists refer to the wounding of the slave of the high priest as Peter, with impetuous zeal, struck savagely in what he thought was defense of his Master. His purpose was to cut off a head, not sever an ear. This incident, involving the use of a sword and Jesus' comment thereupon, has a bearing on the attitude of our Lord toward war.[7] However, only Luke records a healing, and this, of course, has created a very genuine problem. Dr. Abbott has an ingenious suggestion that this miracle of surgery is due to a misunderstanding on the part of Luke of some ambiguous word used in Christ's command to Peter, "Restore it [the sword] to its place," and that Luke interpreted the restoration as applying to the ear.[8] Even though Luke "dearly loves a good miracle," in the phrase of Professor Percy Gardner, nevertheless, if we had more information the difficulty might be solved.

Luke, followed by John, tells us that it was the *right* ear.

---

[7] See my treatment in the *Anglican Theological Review*, Jan., 1944, p. 42, reprinted in the *British Weekly*, Aug. 24, 1944.

[8] *Classical Review* (1893), quoted in Shafto, *op. cit.*, p. 148.

John's Gospel gives the added information that it was Simon Peter who struck the blow and that the name of the victim was Malchus. The other evangelists identify him simply as the slave of the high priest. Some commentators feel he was the leader of the band. The mention of the name would suggest that this man later became a Christian.

When we study Luke's account carefully, we may be given help. Luke, with the carefulness of a medical man, records that it was the *right* ear. The words "cut off" do not necessarily mean that the ear was severed so that it fell to the ground.[9] The whole incident leads us to believe that this was not the case. The words of Jesus, "Suffer ye thus far," are evidence that his hands were bound or handcuffed. It was a request on the part of our Lord to his captor to permit a work of mercy. Again, the statement, "He touched his ear," is an indication that the member was not completely severed. Granted that this was the case, any good surgeon, under the circumstances, would have replaced the ear. If it were bandaged carefully, there was a chance for normal healing. The record in Luke is such that it is entirely possible no miracle is meant other than that of the normal healing of a wound which was assisted by the careful return of the hanging member to its place by Jesus. If the above analysis is correct, it would account for the other evangelists' not mentioning a miracle. Whether there was an actual miracle in this instance or not, the skillful hands of our Lord were employed to good purpose.

> There is grace and pow'r in the trying hour,
> In the touch of His hand on mine.[10]

Whatever may have been the facts in the incident, Peter's life was certainly saved by the concern of Jesus for one of those who came to arrest him, for in that day any such show of force toward an officer who represented the law would have meant

[9] Bernard, *op. cit.*, II, 589.
[10] Used by permission Hope Publishing Co.

that a life would have been forfeited for a wounded ear. In the high moment of our Lord's own jeopardy his first thought was for others.

In some ways the most modern of all surgery is plastic surgery. We today know that there is a valid and an increasing place for it as we recognize the positive personality changes any abnormal appearance makes. What we have discovered Jesus instinctively knew. On the surface this story seems rather incidental. Yet there is something about it that brought forth immediate response on the part of early Christians. It is by no chance that all four gospel writers tell it. Perhaps unconsciously, they recorded it to show that our Lord was interested in the whole man—his external appearance as well as the health of his body and soul.

Jesus responded to the need for physical hearing of those who were deaf. With ringing enthusiasm he exclaimed, "If any man have ears to hear, let him hear." There are ears that do not hear, as he said on more than one occasion. They have become so accustomed to the sound of suffering that it no longer registers. Too often men do not want it to register because if it did they would have to respond. They are "good" men who have to live with themselves. To the cry for help that falls upon their physical ear they give immediate and often sacrificial attention. But when it comes from farther afield—across the railroad tracks or across the ocean—that is another matter. As vital Christians must we not recognize the ease with which we raise psychic barriers to the appeal for aid, understanding that this can become an escape mechanism for us lest we be convicted and realize that we must give aid beyond our present commitments? One of the outstanding Christian requirements for our generation is a consecrated imagination. In blood, sweat, toil, and tears men of our day are discovering what the greathearts of all ages have known: "No man is an *Iland*, intire of it selfe; every man is a peece of the

*Continent*, a part of the *maine*." [11] It is true for nations as well as for individuals. That we are recognizing it is one of the most hopeful facts for the future. In our time Christians must be in the vanguard of the helpful. We must be extremely keen in our response to the cry of suffering, even though it is so great and arises so constantly that one tends to become calloused to human need, feeling that it is impossible to help everywhere, and so why become alarmed anywhere? Our cue in this connection is to remember that Jesus always gave the help that he could in the circumstance in which he found himself. He did not heal all the ears in Jerusalem or all the lepers in Israel any more than did Elisha in the days of Naaman—but he knew that he had a responsibility for giving help when he could. Jesus constantly maintained his sensitiveness to every human need; so should his followers. It is that note which appeals to Christians in the song which Ira Sankey popularized two generations ago:

> But none of the ransomed ever knew
>   How deep were the waters crossed;
> Nor how dark was the night that the Lord passed thro'
>   Ere He found His sheep that was lost.
> Out in the desert He heard its cry—
>   So sick and so helpless and ready to die.

Our Lord heard the cry. Certainly he wants his disciples likewise to have ears that hear.

[11] John Donne.

# 13

## Vision for the Blind

FOR CENTURIES blindness has been one of the scourges and curses of the Orient. In Palestine and Egypt, I have been shocked to see little children playing unconcernedly in dung while a ring of flies and gnats literally surrounded their eyes. Yet the prevalence of blindness does not alleviate in any degree the tragedy that it brings to those involved. As with any man of sympathy, Jesus could not see it and fail to be moved with compassion. There is evidence in the Gospels that he restored sight to many who were so afflicted. The four accounts treated at length include John's record of the man born blind (9:1-41),[1] Matthew's story of the healing of two blind men (9:27-31), the blind man of Bethsaida (Mark 8:22-26), and the account of the restoration of sight to blind Bartimaeus (Matt. 20:29-34; Mark 10:46-52; Luke 18:35-43).

Man has always had a passion to see. First he uses the eyes with which he was born. With them he sees the wonders of God's earth about him with all the glory of it, but still man is not satisfied. He wants to see the unseeable, so he invents the telescope to look beyond the night and bring new stars and galaxies into his vision. He develops the microscope to observe the tiny world beneath his normal range of vision. In the modern age of electronics and out of the very agony of war he invented radar, with its uncanny ability to see through fog, smoke, or night. All these are man's efforts to extend his vision. With such

---

[1] To be treated separately in the next chapter.

148

a passion to extend normal vision, how much more must be a man's desire to see should that be denied him by blindness? It was Jesus who taught us that seeing is not always observing the physical. "They have eyes and see not," he said. All men want to see with their physical eyes. Good men must have spiritual vision as well. After John Milton had gone blind, he wrote the following lines that became prophetic of the keener spiritual sight that God granted him:

> Thus with the year
> Seasons return; but not to me returns
> Day, or the sweet approach of even or morn,
> Or sight of vernal bloom, or summer's rose,
> Or flocks, or herds, or human face divine;
> But cloud instead and ever-during dark
> Surrounds me. . . .
>
> .    .    .    .    .    .    .    .
>
> So much the rather thou, Celestial Light,
> Shine inward, and the mind through all her powers
> Irradiate; there plant eyes; all mist from thence
> Purge and disperse, that I may see and tell
> Of things invisible to mortal sight.[2]

## I. The Healing of Two Blind Men—*Matt. 9:27-31*

Many students of the gospel see this incident as a duplication of Matt. 20:29-34, where we have the account of restoration of sight for two blind men. In both records there are two men; both men call on Jesus as the "son of David" and ask for pity. In each account Jesus asked a question to spur faith; he touched their eyes as he spoke of their faith. Finally, their eyes were opened. We observe that all of the essential factors in both accounts are the same.[3] When we know how the Gospels were written, we see it is entirely possible that both accounts refer to the same situation. However, this is not an inevitable explanation,

[2] *Paradise Lost*, Book III.
[3] See McNeile, *op. cit.*, p. 128.

149

because the Gospels themselves are witness to the fact that there were unrecorded instances of restoration of sight to those who were blind. In Matt. 9, Jesus admonishes the two not to broadcast the boon that had been given them. Jesus faced constantly the problem of people being so excited by a healing that his normal activity of teaching became well-nigh impossible. Today we get some small indication of what can happen in such circumstances when there is a report in Roman Catholic circles of some remarkable occurrence. Contrary to the request of Jesus, "they, when they were departed, spread abroad his fame in all that country." In Matt. 20 the account simply says, "They followed him." The emphasis in both accounts is upon faith. Jesus touched "their eyes, saying, According to your faith be it unto you. And their eyes were opened."

If men were as active in spreading the news of spiritual benefits as of physical, the famous slogan of the Student Volunteer Movement, "The world for Christ in this generation," would come true. The miracles had their place in the life of our Lord —"Believe me for the very works' sake"—but the fundamental genius of Jesus is seen in the fact that he convinced his followers that his program and ministry were spiritual and so fired them with zeal to impart this truth to others that they "spread his fame" throughout the whole of the Mediterranean world.

Among the supreme glories of Christianity are its reproductive vitality and its proof that the success of its message does not depend upon physical cures but upon spiritual change. We need especially in this day to recognize that life can be vigorous and even beautiful without the ability to reproduce itself, but that a faith that does not transmit its essence to the next generation is soon dead, no matter how charming it might be in our time. In the animal world the mule is a very effective draft creature, but it has been said that it is "without pride of ancestry or hope of posterity." The Ethiopian eunuch in Acts had risen to great prominence in his realm; he had spiritual vitality of the first rank, but he could never have a son. However, he did have the ability to transmit his faith to others in his land, so there has been a continuous Christian history in Ethiopia from his day to the present. In our time there is a spiritual life that is nonreproductive. Some people have the new birth; they serve Christ effectively; they do many good deeds; they live beautiful Christian lives; but they do not reproduce themselves spiritually. Whole areas of Christianity have been marked by a low spiritual birthrate. The marks of a vital Christian are almost measured by the zeal with which he shares his faith. "Every branch in me that beareth not fruit he taketh away." The zeal to share a physical boon is understandable, but lasting change for men will come only as we share with the non-Christian world the benefits and the challenges offered by the Christian way of life. This is the reason the great forward movements in the history of the Church have been those ages marked by evangelistic and missionary advance. In speaking of Christian advance on the American frontier Kenneth Latourette says:

In general, Methodists were relatively stronger north of the Ohio River and the Baptists were stronger in the South. Yet both won so prominent a place in the West that, when it was no longer a frontier, they remained the largest of the Protestant groups. This was probably because by their zeal in carrying the Christian message to the unchurched and especially to the rank and file, they appealed to what was the nearest approach to a proletariat in the older American stock. [4]

In days gone by, great power was considered to reside in the touch of a mighty or a good man. According to both Suetonius [5] and Tacitus [6] the Emperor Vespasian restored sight after a mechanical process accompanied by a touch.[7] In medieval England the king's touch was considered to be a potent cure for

[4] *The Great Century* ("A History of the Expansion of Christianity," Vol. 4), p. 186.
[5] *Vespas* 7.
[6] *History* IV. 81.
[7] See above, p. 142.

scrofula. In the gospel account of the woman who touched the hem of his garment, Jesus immediately turned and asked the question, "Who touched me?" We would expect our Lord to use the methods of healing that would promote faith on the part of the one he was helping.

Sight was restored to these two because of their faith. Faith is always the prerequisite for healing or restoration, faith on the part of either the sufferer or those near him. Someone must exercise this great gift. Recall by contrast the account which says that in certain localities Jesus "did not many mighty works there because of their unbelief." As with many of the works of healing, Jesus urged that it not be publicized because of the popular excitement this would naturally occasion, making his spiritual ministry more difficult.

## II. THE BLIND MAN OF BETHSAIDA—*Mark 8:22-26*

Mark alone gives us the rather striking incident of the healing of the blind man at Bethsaida. There is a close parallel in this story with Mark's previous miracle of healing the deaf mute in 7:32-37. In both accounts saliva and touch are the methods employed. The use of saliva as a healing agent has been discussed in connection with the latter account.[8] Bethsaida was a village upon which Jesus pronounced judgment because of the failure of the men of that city to repent (Matt. 11:21). As a community, Bethsaida had failed; the men of this town had lost their great opportunity. They had forgotten that

> There is a tide in the affairs of men,
> Which, taken at the flood, leads on to fortune;
> Omitted, all the voyage of their life
> Is bound in shallows and in miseries. [9]

Nevertheless, individuals could be saved out of the community.

[8] See above, p. 142.
[9] Shakespeare, *Julius Caesar*, Act IV, scene 3.

However, it is interesting to observe that Jesus did not restore sight to the blind man within the city environs. Our Lord took him by the hand and led him out of the village. There may be an implication here that Bethsaida was in such spiritual blackness that had the blind man's eyes been opened within its walls, he still could not have seen.

Envision for a moment the most remarkable walk which that blind man ever took. Beside him was the firm, confident step of the rabbi from Nazareth. The soft hand of the blind man, who could do nothing but beg, was grasped firmly by the large rough hand of the Carpenter. The confidence of a dawning faith must have been transmitted through those clasped hands. The incident brings to our minds the words of the psalmist, "Yea, though I walk through the valley of deep darkness, thou art with me," and such hymns as "He Leadeth Me" or "Where He Leads Me I Will Follow." One would give much to know of the conversation that took place between the blind man and his virile Companion. Of one thing we are sure: the man learned much from Jesus, and our Lord, as does any good physician, learned much about his patient. It is certain that during and after the walk spiritual light dawned with great glory in the heart of the blind man.

Then came the time for the restoration of his vision. With saliva Jesus anointed the sightless eyes, laying his hands on them. He asked, "Do you see anything?" The man replied, "I see men as trees, walking." [10] A modern oculist is always careful about the readmission of light to the retina. Our Lord would be no less careful when there was need. The account is clear that the man's vision was at first blurred; but blurred or not, he began to use the sight which Jesus had given him.

So it is with spiritual sight. When it first comes, it is often

[10] Some commentators see a parallel to Hellenistic stories of healing. There is an inscription of a cure in the temple of Asclepius, in which it is said that the first things seen were the trees in the temple area. However, some similarity does not necessarily make a parallel. See Branscomb, *op. cit.*, p. 142.

blurred, but if we use the measure of truth that is ours, finally clarity and understanding come. When Paul sent the runaway Onesimus back to his master, Philemon, neither Paul nor Philemon spoke against slavery. However, Paul did something much more significant. He counseled Philemon to treat Onesimus as a brother—and that is using the spiritual vision which he had.

Jesus again put his hands upon the eyes of the man, the record tells us, "and made him look up: and he was restored, and saw every man clearly." Here is a clear indication of progressive restoration. In the beginning Jesus had effected a partial cure, but he was not satisfied, nor would the man have been satisfied. Chrysostom, with a typically archaic but fascinating interpretation, finds the reason for the progressive cure in the imperfectness of the man's faith.[11] Jesus counsels him not even to enter into the village, for, despite the wonder of the deed, the men of Bethsaida were evidently so hard of heart that they would not believe.

### III. Blind Bartimaeus—*Mark 10:46-52; Luke 18:35-43; Matt. 20:29-34*

The most dramatic of these instances is that of Timaeus, son of Timaeus. The Hebrew, using a prefix to show the relation, called him Bartimaeus.[12] Vivid as is the record, there is no attempt to make the case appear as wondrous as possible. It is simple, straightforward reporting. Matthew makes a difficulty by saying two blind men. Harmonists have contended that Mark and Luke tell about the most important one. Luke places the incident at the entrance to Jericho, while Matthew and Mark locate it at the departure from the city. Luke is not so concerned with chronology. Some commentators have felt that he placed the incident as he did because it made a good introduction to the story of Zacchaeus.[13] Should we be expecting complete

[11] Trench, *op. cit.*, p. 386 (1887 ed.).
[12] Many Bible students say that Matthew's account in 9:27-31 is a duplication of this incident. This possibility has already been discussed in this chapter.
[13] Creed, *op. cit.*, p. 228.

biblical harmony, it is a fact that in the time of Jesus there were two towns, the ancient site of Jericho and the one rebuilt by Herod.[14] So if one is attempting to explain all biblical difficulties, it is entirely possible that all three of the writers were correct, each giving the account from his particular viewpoint. Some of the best and most devout scholars have long since ceased trying to resolve every apparent discrepancy in the gospel record, both because of their knowledge as to how the Gospels were compiled and because of their recognition that our information, at best, is fragmentary and that if we had more knowledge the problems would in many cases take care of themselves.

Following Mark's account we find Bartimaeus sitting beside the road when he became aware of an important procession passing. Learning that it was Jesus of Nazareth, he immediately cried out and asked for mercy. His chance had come, and with insistence he was making the most of it. As we would expect of any blind man, the first thing he wanted was restoration of vision. In the light of the problem which we have, whether at the entrance or the exit to Jericho, one might observe that what Bartimaeus wanted to know was where he was. The chaos so typical of much of today's life is due to the fact that modern man has not the faintest idea where he is spiritually. Irving Babbitt could well remark, "Unless there is a reaffirmation of the truths of the inner life in some form—religious or humanistic—civilization is threatened at the base."

Notice the possessiveness of the crowd. They knew the mass excitement that came from following a famous rabbi. With typical collective self-importance they tried to silence the noisy blind man, but even more insistently he cried, "Jesus, thou son of David, have mercy on me." Only here in Mark and Luke is Jesus called "son of David," though this is a frequent title in Matthew. "Son of David" is very definitely a messianic title, but publicly to proclaim Jesus as such, as Major points out, is

[14] *International Standard Bible Encyclopedia*, p. 1592.

155

treason, as it "might easily suggest to the Roman authorities the signal of revolt." [15] This was the reason the crowd tried to silence the man, but it was Bartimaeus' golden opportunity, and he would not let it pass. Then again he very likely could have felt that the messianic title would be pleasing to Jesus. The incident impressed the beholders. The enthusiasm of the crowd in Luke 18:43 is a good background for the subsequent acclaim in connection with the triumphal entry. Word of the messianic title and its acceptance by Jesus could easily have been carried to Pilate. "Jesus for the first time steps out openly to the front of the stage and deliberately chooses the part of a public character." [16]

Bartimaeus would not be put off; Jesus of Nazareth was passing by.

> Pass me not, O gentle Saviour,
>   Hear my humble cry;
> While on others thou art calling,
>   Do not pass me by.

He may have been physically blind, but his spiritual sight was keen. He had heard enough of the Nazarene to persuade him that this man must be the Son of David. Whether his shouting was treason or no, did not so much concern him. He wanted to recover his sight, and he believed profoundly that the Messiah, the Son of David, would do something for him. It has been observed that though the story is in past time, it is eternal in truth. Bartimaeus represents the soul of humanity as it gropes for light, while Jesus is the light of the world, and in him is no darkness at all.[17] The most insistent quality of light is its immediate and complete pervasiveness. When the sun is shining, all one needs do to have light is raise the shade, and the room is instantly filled with

[15] Major, Manson, and Wright, *op. cit.*, p. 136.
[16] Robinson, *op. cit.*, p. 169.
[17] Lang, *op. cit.*, p. 238.

light. When Jesus of Nazareth is passing by, all one needs to do is ask, and he will have sight, both physical and spiritual.

There is a very significant variant reading in the Sinaitic Syriac, an ancient gospel translation. When Jesus asked him what he wished, our common version says, "The blind man said unto him, Lord, that I might receive my sight." This is the answer we would expect, but the Sinaitic Syriac has "That I might see thee." Religiously, of course, the latter is the most significant statement. If we apply the rule of textual criticism which says that the most difficult reading is probably correct, there is much to be said for this version. Either way, recovery of sight meant seeing Jesus! And that was the fact above all facts devoutly to be desired.

The great rabbi had noticed Bartimaeus! The crowd at once, and typically, shifts in its attitude. A moment ago this blind beggar was a nuisance; now he has the attention of Jesus. The same self-appointed spokesman who had said, with a sense of importance, "Be quiet," now exclaimed, "Be of good comfort, rise; he calleth thee." Many a sermon has been preached with this as a text. The blind man cared for none of these things. He simply seized his moment, arose, flung away his garment in his haste to get near the Son of David, and came to Jesus. Notice the unconscious vividness and artistry here. Instead of using the phrase "son of David"—that phrase which carried the connotation of majesty and greatness—he changed to the endearing "*Rabboni*"—My dear great one—a term of affection used by a pupil of his master. In contrast with Mark's other story of restoration of sight (8:22-26) here the healing is with a word alone. As with Matthew's two accounts (9:27-31 and 20:29-34), the center of interest is upon the faith of the man who would not be denied help when he knew Jesus was near. The account says that after recovering his sight he followed Jesus in the way.

The world needs a clear vision of Jesus so that it may recover its sight and its sanity. One thinks of the famous words of Lecky in his *History of European Morals*, where he says, "The simple record of these three short years of active life has done more to regenerate and soften mankind than all the disquisitions of philosophers and all the exhortations of moralists. This has been the well-spring of whatever is best and purest in the Christian life."

Blaise Pascal was one of the greatest scientists who ever lived. He was a genius of the first rank, at eleven writing a treatise on sound, at sixteen one on conic sections that astounded Parisian mathematicians. His major scientific discovery was the principle of fluid pressure now known as Pascal's law. However, Pascal is known to posterity as much for his religious understanding as for his scientific ability. As he meditated upon God's ways with man, he developed his famous "wager": if a man must gamble, let him gamble upon the fact of God and eternal life, for he has everything to gain and nothing to lose. As a comparatively young man while meditating upon the seventeenth chapter of John a great mystical experience came to him that he considered such a famous discovery that he wrote it down and sewed it up within his jacket, where it was discovered after his death: "God of Abraham, God of Isaac, God of Jacob, not of the philosophers and scholars. God of Jesus Christ. Thy God shall be my God. . . . Let me never be separated from him." [18]

The outstanding discovery our scientific age can make is not the method for the release of atomic energy, but that God is the God of the living, and most of all of men like Jesus of Nazareth, who gave to the world a clear vision of the true, the good, and the beautiful. Here is spiritual sight and understanding. Like the once-blind man the world needs to look to Jesus and start to follow him in the way.

[18] Emile Cailliet, *Pascal*, p. 131.

# 14

## Now I See

OF ALL human afflictions blindness strikes the most responsive chord of sympathy. For most of humanity, darkness and night mean a cessation of activity, a time when life is lived at its lowest ebb. True, darkness brings blessed rest, but the rest is designed to give strength for the morrow when the day is at hand. Men live for light; they work in the light; without the light they are helpless. If the night continues too long, they may even become hopeless.

Man's sight is his most cherished physical faculty. The loss or lack of it is a tragedy beyond comparison. Not only does man hold and long for physical sight, but he looks forward to that day when he shall no longer see through a glass darkly but face to face, when spiritual vision will match the reality of physical sight. An aged Negro was once asked, "What is the first thing you are going to do when you get to heaven?" His woolly, grayed head bowed for a moment, and then he raised his dark face, wrinkled with the years. A wistful expressiveness came into his eyes as he replied, "I'se jest gonna sit down for a thousand years and *look* at Jesus!" His fondest desire was to see Jesus as he is, a wish shared with many another follower of the Master.

One day Jesus and his disciples were walking and talking together, as was their custom (John 9:1-41). The point of time in John appears to make an immediate connection with the preceding chapter, yet the tone is different from Chapter 8. Chapters 9 and 10 are definitely to be taken together. In the latter the Feast of Dedication is mentioned (vs. 22). Consequently it is likely that Chapter 9 starts a new section in the narrative.[1] It is entirely possible that the rabbi from Nazareth and his disciples had just come from the temple and were either still within its confines or not far removed. Likely they had gone to the temple for special prayer or worship, for this was the Sabbath day. The university of Jesus was one of the open sky, the broad fields, or the busy streets. The passing incident of the locality or the moment would often form the background for a case study. Such was true on this day.

A familiar man, blind from birth, sat in his accustomed spot begging. It is the only gospel incident in which it is stated that a man born blind was given sight. Some scholars see in this John's penchant for heightening the miraculous, yet it is typical of John to take the most outstanding incident of a certain class and portray that. There is vividness to the story because of the statement that the man had always been blind. Much of the narrative depends on the latter fact. The man's predicament gave rise to an old and familiar theological question which the disciples now asked, "Who did sin, this man, or his parents, that he was born blind?" The sins of the fathers visited upon the children could account for the latter part of the question, but what about the former? How could a man *born* blind sin and thereby cause his own blindness? Some of the rabbis had speculated about a pre-existent state,[2] which fact might account for the peculiarity of the question. Then, certain rabbis taught that sin could be committed even in one's mother's womb, as witnessed by the prenatal struggle between Jacob and Esau.

The disciples wanted light on the age-old problem of evil and the human suffering that grows out of evil. The accepted Jewish solution for the problem of evil was that it was a direct result of sin.[3] There has always been wisdom in this view, for in all

[1] Bernard, *op. cit.*, II, 323; see also Macgregor, *op. cit.*, p. 224.
[2] Wisdom of Solomon 8:20, "Being good, I came into a body undefiled."
[3] In Luke 13:1-5, Jesus refutes this idea.

likelihood the vast bulk of human misery is caused by human sin. The answer was obvious when one could see the sins of a father visited upon his children, or when iniquity in one's own life brought swift and dire calamity. The judgment of the Jew that sin brings evil needs to be re-emphasized in this modern day which has made all too light of iniquity. That all suffering and its resultant evil are caused by sin is the problem with which Job wrestled. The disciples, in the very wording of their question, showed that they too had some misgivings about the matter. Today we probably know more of the answers to this question than did Job. We know that suffering is often part of life as it is. If the baby is to walk, it must risk the danger of falling and subsequent injury which might ensue. In such a figure as Abraham Lincoln we find the ashes of suffering become the catalyst for helping to build a noble character. Probably the best and most Christian of answers is that which Jesus gives in its essence here in this very passage. Out of suffering can come a greater good. "Neither hath this man sinned, nor his parents: but *that the works of God should be made manifest in him.*"

This is one of seven stupendous miracles recorded in the Fourth Gospel. The seven are symbolic. John states Jesus worked many more miracles than these. Each one of the seven is designed to show some especially remarkable ability of Jesus. John admits frankly that he is writing with a purpose, "that ye might believe that Jesus is the Christ" (20:31). Notice the outstanding character of each one of the miracles recorded in John: changing of the water into wine (2:1-11), healing of the nobleman's son (4:46-54), healing of the impotent man (5:2-9), feeding of the five thousand (6:4-13), walking on the water (6:16-21) healing of the man born blind (9:1-41), and the raising of Lazarus (11:1-44). Some are recorded in the other Gospels, but the supernatural power is such in these seven that no rationalistic or naturalistic explanation could possibly account for what took place. Alan Richardson has well pointed out:

Thus, even if St. John warns us against the danger of believing that the importance of the miracles resides in their impressiveness as wonders, he does not allow us to overlook the fact that the miracles of Jesus *were* miracles, and not mere symbolic actions which *any* prophet might have performed. They are "the works which none other did." [4]

Apart from the fact of miracle, in the entire gospel story there is no record of more intrinsic credibility than the ninth chapter of John. Its vividness and detail are in sharpest focus. A. E. Garvie says, "The narrative in Chapter 9 makes a convincing impression of historical reality." [5] The account has the genuine ring of an actual life situation with its explosive tensions. A. T. Olmstead, who is anything but naïve in his general views, writes:

Were not this an account of a miraculous healing, we should have had no hesitation in accepting it as completely authentic. Certainly it is no dead production of a professional writer of formal literature; it has the "feel" of genuine life, even to a somewhat robust humor. [6]

C. J. Wright adds:

It is permissible to believe that the author is using some historical tradition, as a narrative framework, for the fuller presentation of the mind of Jesus. He is not, that is, inventing a story. [7]

Apart from the miracle, the more one studies the framework of the story, the more one is impressed with its life-situation reality. Yet the remarkable thing about the story is that it is quite pointless unless sight was brought to the blind man. Jesus could have made a categorical statement that the man's affliction was not due to sin. He could also have gone on and spoken concerning the necessity of working during the day. He might

[4] *Op. cit.*, p. 116.
[5] *Abingdon Bible Commentary*, p. 1078.
[6] *Op. cit.*, pp. 154-55.
[7] Major, Manson, and Wright, *op. cit.*, p. 811.

even have talked in the high theological language which John ascribes to him, but the conversation of the man, his controversy with his accusers, are meaningless apart from the thing that happened to him. He did not feel that he was in a position to express a conviction regarding the person of the healer, but he said, "One thing I know, that, whereas I was blind, now I see."

Even a casual reading of the passage points to the fact that the whole incident begins and is wrapped up in the discourse, "The Light of the World." Down the ages prophets, seers, philosophers, and poets have given us a tiny glimmer of light.

> How far that little candle throws its beams!
> So shines a good deed in a naughty world.

The Quaker seer, George Fox, could say, "I saw also that there was an ocean of darkness and death, but an infinite ocean of light and love, which flowed over the ocean of darkness: and in that also I saw the infinite love of God." [8] That light and love we best see in Jesus, whom Christians delight to call "the sun of righteousness."

> The whole world was lost in the darkness of sin;
> The Light of the world is Jesus.

"The Light of the world." How full of meaning is this metaphor! Day is the time for work; light is necessary for work and for the world. It is quite understandable why some primitive people worshiped the sun because the sun was the giver of light and comfort to warm mankind and coax the earth into bringing forth abundantly the harvest of food necessary to his sustenance.

"I must work the works of him that sent me, while it is day: the night cometh, when no man can work. As long as I am in the world, I am the light of the world." (John 9:4-5.) Here we have the utmost in human self-esteem bordering on the arrogant, or we have divine truth. Only upon the lips of Jesus of Nazareth

[8] *Journal* (bicentenary ed., 1891), p. 19.

do these words not seem out of character. They are nonetheless remarkable if we hold, as do many good and devout scholars, that they are interpretative expressions put into the mouth of Jesus by the author of the Gospel. Time has proved the veracity of the words. Jesus is the light of the world. Verse 4 is tied up so closely with verse 5 that the intrinsic probability of the former carries the latter with it. Today is the day. Jesus knew, as few men have known, that we must do our work in the God-given moment which is the present. Our light must be put on a candlestick, not hidden under a bushel measure. Jesus never heard of existentialism, but he was fully aware that God's supreme adverb of time is NOW. "The kingdom of God is *at hand*." His task was to bring spiritual light to eyes that were in great darkness. One can never understand the full mystical qualities in the nature of Jesus of Nazareth until one has got into the heart and spirit of the Fourth Gospel. The quest for the historic Jesus will never be complete apart from the new appreciation of the nature of our Lord that we find in John.[9]

Jesus made a paste of clay and saliva, with which he anointed the eyes of the blind man. Apparently the man had not asked for healing. This is unlike the synoptic narratives, but is not at all improbable in the light of the story. To John the light which is Jesus cannot but shine. A philosophical and theological question can be raised in connection with all of the mighty works wrought by Jesus: If he had such power and such divine love,

[9] New Testament research has yet to say the last word on the whole problem of John's Gospel. Back of the four-document hypothesis, back of form criticism, back of the oral tradition, stand the men who walked with our Lord and originally gave his words to the world. Papias, in a famous passage, tells us that Mark listened to the preaching of Peter and wrote down faithfully the things which he heard. New Testament scholarship has widely accepted this statement as correct. Peter's sermons therefore become the source for most of Mark's material. The eminently practical Peter gives his interpretation of Jesus as a noble and true prophet, who could not be holden of death. Faith in this Jesus brings forgiveness of sin. Yet without John's account the rich mystical nature which our Lord must have possessed would be little known to us. Some modern scholars are seeing an increasing credibility in John's record. See A. T. Olmstead, *Jesus in the Light of History*.

why stop with healing one or two blind men or paralytics? In the face of so much sickness and misery, to help the few is like trying to bail out the ocean with a bucket. The answer lies in the very nature of the Incarnation. God in Christ limited or "emptied" himself, as Paul phrased it. As the incarnate Son of God, Jesus was constrained by his very humanity. As long as men were to remain men, mass healing would have to wait upon modern medicine, coupled with the will to heal given by the spirit of Jesus. In the meantime one must do what one can "while it is day"—in the age and with the means which he has. We must meet every opportunity for doing what we can to alleviate suffering and sickness.

But we shall never do our part, either to individuals or on a large scale, until we apprehend that it is only through us and others that God works, and that when we pass by a needy person, we prevent God's love from reaching him and disappoint the purpose of God. . . . To however few a number and in however small a way we are the media through which God finds His love to men.[10]

Do you remember the film story of Pierre and Marie Curie? They had made 487 experiments to try to separate radium from pitchblende. All had failed. In despair Pierre said, "It can't be done; it can't be done! Maybe in a hundred years it can be done, but never in our lifetime."

Madame Curie showed her greatness by responding, "If it takes a hundred years, it will be a pity, but I dare not do less than work for it so long as I have life."

The question of the disciples, "Who sinned . . . ?" centered attention on the man's situation. The resulting discourse on the light of the world would be more meaningful to the disciples if the action of Jesus was the immediate means for light entering the blind man's darkened eyes. The method our Lord employed was not unusual in the first century. Saliva from the mouth of a man who was fasting was considered to be of especial value in

[10] Marcus Dods, *The Gospel of St. John* ("The Expositor's Bible"), I, 309-10.

cases of eye trouble.[11] We have already mentioned that Suetonius and Tacitus record an incident of a healing by the Emperor Vespasian using this particular method. Jesus employed it in two other instances, one in the case of a blind man (Mark 8:23) and another in connection with a deaf mute (Mark 7:33). The complete reliance upon his heavenly Father which Jesus exhibited on other occasions would indicate that he himself did not place any special emphasis upon the physical anointing. But as Jesus was both a wise and a good man, plus a master in the use of psychology, he certainly recognized that he had to begin at the place where men were if he was to help them. It is entirely likely that Jesus knew that such an anointing would help to awaken faith in the subject. Here was a healer with a wide reputation who was doing something definite in the case of this blind man. The blind man himself recognized the very unusual nature of the cure. With the facts given in the record it is not possible for us to account for what took place, except to attribute it to the remarkable power Jesus possessed through faith in God. Unscientific? No, for we are at last beginning to realize that there is a far closer connection between the physical and the spiritual than appeared to nineteenth-century investigators. We now know that faith and science are not in conflict, for physical research is increasingly demonstrating that we live in a universe where "faith has its scientific means and science has its foundation in faith."

After the application of the ointment Jesus said to the patient, "Go, wash in the pool of Siloam." With some degree of confidence the man did as he was bid. The record itself gives the translation of this word Siloam, "Which is by interpretation, sent" (9:7). The insertion of this comment into the text is a clear indication that there is some play upon the word *sent*, suggesting that an allegorical interpretation is to be understood. In John's eyes Christ was himself the one "sent" by God. From

[11] Major, Manson, and Wright, *op. cit.*, p. 813.

Chrysostom's time on there have been many different explanations. Chrysostom himself felt that the name symbolized Christ, who was "sent" of God. Bruce, who finds no difficulty in accepting the fact of the miracle, nevertheless believes that an allegorical interpretation is bound up in the actual healing. He calls it an acted parable, the clay symbolizing the effect of Pharisaic teaching which blinds, whereas the sending to Siloam is a symbol of the counteracting influence of Christ.[12] Jesus gave sight to the physically blind, but he was far more interested in opening the eyes of the spiritually blind. He uses the metaphor again and again as he speaks of the necessity for spiritual vision for those "who have eyes and see not." Other scholars have seen some connection between the washing and Christian baptism. According to this view it is the author's way of pointing out that the rite of the sacrament of baptism is essential to healing and spiritual sight. There is a definite reminiscence of the command of Elisha to Naaman to wash in the Jordan if he wished to be cured of his leprosy (II Kings 5:1-14).

Dr. Olmstead gives a vivid description of the journey taken by the man:

In imagination we may watch the blind man hurrying along the road which from west of the Temple walls descended the Cheesemaker's Valley under the viaduct leading to the Hasmonean Palace. It was a fine road, twenty-five to fifty feet wide from curb to curb, and paved by Herod's orders with great blocks of hard whitish limestone. Now and then he would stumble over the manholes, projecting a foot and a half above the pavement, which permitted cleaning of the drain below. Leaving on the right the main road leading on to the southern gate, the blind man felt his way, right hand on the rock of the scarp, down thirty-four monumental steps of alternate broad and narrow tread. Turning left through an opening in a low parapet, he was sheltered by the covered arcade which surrounded the pool, seventy-five by seventy-one feet on the side. In a court to the south, he prepared to take his bath, and then bathed

[12] *Op. cit.*, p. 204.

in the water brought from Gihon's spring under the rock of Ophel by Hezekiah's aqueduct.[13]

After following carefully the instruction of Jesus the man "came seeing." [14] Physical eyes were opened for the first time, and the wonders of an entirely new world swam into the comprehension of this man, who all of his life had known nothing but bleak blackness. Once the greatest fact in his life had been his blindness; now the supreme fact in all the universe was that he saw.

Marvelous as was the case of healing, the most interesting part of the whole story follows the cure. The blind man's sight was restored on the Sabbath. To the strict legalists of that day the mixing of the ointment constituted work. Consequently they considered it a violation of the Sabbath. It made little difference to them whether a man could see or not. The incident happening on the Sabbath was a powder train that led off into a discussion of the antecedents and the present authority of the healer. At first the opponents endeavored to establish the fact of fraud between Jesus and the man. This was not really the blind man at all, but one who looked like him. This effort was made of none effect by the parents, who established the identity of the man. Two witnesses agreed that this was their son, and he had been born blind. Here the difference is between "the Pharisees," who were later called "the Jews," and the parents of the man. The controversy is *about* Jesus, though he is not himself present. Still he is "the invisible mind which dominates the situation." [15]

The man's parents are brought somewhat unwittingly into the picture. They fear for their place in the synagogue, but still they speak with a degree of courage, plus some admixture of wonderment that the Pharisees are so blind as not to know who healed their son.

[13] *Op. cit.,* p. 152.

[14] Bernard suggests that some days may have elapsed between vss. 7 and 8— time for the neighbors to realize that a change had taken place in the man's condition (*op. cit.,* II, 329).

[15] Major, Manson, and Wright, *op. cit.,* p. 815.

There is a fascinating advance in the faith of the man himself. When he was originally asked, "How were your eyes opened?" he responded, "The *man* called Jesus made clay and anointed my eyes . . . , so I . . . received my sight." The accusers now began an insistent train of questions designed to confuse and to condemn, not to gain knowledge. Again they wanted to know how he had received his sight. Rather patiently the blind man explained once more the method and what took place. The Pharisees now resorted to a priori reasoning. They started out, "This man is not from God, for he does not keep the sabbath." Of course, there was division because of the remarkable character of what took place. "Others said, 'How can a man who is a sinner do such signs?' " The point of collusion is raised, but the parents' testimony proves this is out of the question. They are anxious to avoid responsibility, and yet there is an undercurrent of defiant faith in their answer.

The author of the account, with dramatic intensity, leads up to the problem of the person of the healer. "What do you say about him?" The blind man, partly as a result of the badgering, partly because the questions were clarifying things in his own mind, replied, *"He is a prophet."* [16] With vindictiveness they demanded that he tell the truth. "Give God the praise [an adjuration to tell the truth]; we know that this man is a sinner." Such blindness struck the once physically blind man with amazement. "Whether he is a sinner, I do not know; one thing I know, that though I was blind, now I see." He was coolly and righteously sarcastic. In continuing the efforts to trap the man his opponents again asked him how he was healed. The man had had enough of their unseemly efforts to discredit the one who had given him such a boon, and replied, "I have told you already, and you would not listen. Why do you want to hear it

---

[16] Notice he did not say *the prophet*. In early Christian circles Jesus is not referred to as *the prophet*, save in John 6:14. That title is usually reserved for John the Baptist. Jesus himself thought of John the Baptist as "the prophet" (Matt. 11:2-15).

again? Do you too want to become his disciples?" That led to further reviling of Jesus, casting aspersions upon his antecedents with the statement, "We do not know where he comes from." What a reply the healed man gave! "Why, this is a marvel! You do not know *where he comes from*, and yet he opened my eyes." There was nothing left for them to do except to cast him out from their group. They could not put him out of the synagogue; only the Sanhedrin could do that; but their actions threatened him with this dire result. Dr. Wright has given a fine summary of what took place:

When confronted with the traditional beliefs of "the Jews," he stands firmly on the ground of personal experience. Let them *explain* the fact as best they can; he *knows* it. But when they become irritated with his obstinacy, he becomes more persistent and confident. He gains in clearness and conviction as they lose in assurance. As falsehood makes them weak, so truth makes him strong. He indulges in irony at their expense. Their weakness disguises itself in a cloak of scornful disdain. Finally, their disdain is exasperated to the point of fury. There is only one thing left for them to do: they use force—thereby revealing their final weakness. This has been a common way of dealing with minorities which had truth on their side. It was the way by which they afterwards dealt with Jesus. Those who cannot be answered must at least be silenced. Light, however, does not cease to shine because men deny it; nor does the tide cease to flow at their command.[17]

Jesus again enters personally into the situation. He heard the disgraceful way in which the man was treated, and he came to give him aid. Jesus found the man and said, "Do you believe in the Son of man?"[18] Jesus is here definitely using a messianic title. Like other good Jews, the blind man was looking for the Messiah, so he responds, "Who is he, Lord, that I might believe on him?" Jesus then disclosed that he himself is the Messiah.

[17] Major, Manson, and Wright, *op. cit.*, p. 815.
[18] "Son of God" of the King James Version, following late manuscripts, is certainly incorrect.

"You have seen him, and it is he who speaks to you." As a result of his badgering and the clarification of his own faith that followed, plus the final sympathetic word from Jesus, the blind man responded, "Lord, I believe." Here we find a complete cycle of faith for the man once blind and likewise a cycle of faith through which many still go. We start with a *man;* we advance in our understanding until we realize that Jesus is a *prophet.* Our eyes are opened, and we see that he is the *Messiah,* God's gracious gift to the world.

Though the once-blind man was cast out of the company and threatened with excommunication, he was infinitely the gainer, for he was found by truth incarnate. He was ready to dedicate his whole being to the grace which he saw in Jesus. His spiritual as well as his physical eyes were opened, and he was prepared to accept Jesus of Nazareth as God's Messiah, the bringer of light into a very dark world.

> Come to the Light, 'tis shining for thee;
> Sweetly the Light has dawn'd upon me,
> Once I was blind, but now I can see;
> The Light of the world is Jesus.

# 15

## When God Is Near

MOSES, one of the great national and religious leaders of all times, had led a motley and rebellious crowd of ex-slaves out of their Egyptian bondage and through months of wandering in the wilderness. He had received strength from communion with a God who had revealed himself as the eternal living one, the "I Am." Yet there came to Moses a period when he felt that he could not go on without a visible consciousness of the reality of the great God with whom he had joined forces. So, with poignant wistfulness, Moses said, "I beseech thee, shew me thy glory." He wanted to see the face of God and the glory. Centuries later Philip made a somewhat similar request, "Lord, shew us the Father, and it sufficeth us." Men have always wanted to be near God, to see his glory.

On one occasion Jesus intimately connected the presence of God's kingdom with the casting out of devils. In our modern ears it is a strange association. "But if I with the finger of God cast out devils, no doubt the kingdom of God is come upon you." (Luke 11:20.) We ask the question, "Can it be that God is near when demons walk on every hand?" There is not space in this study to go exhaustively into the matter of demonism. The name we give it or the philosophy we have about it is relatively unimportant. Account for it as we may, we do find in our world this phenomenon that can be explained by the term "demonism," as well as by more modern psychological terminology. In New Testament days demonism brought tragedy to individuals; today it infects whole societies. Whatever we may call it and however we may think about it, demonism appears to come in cycles through human history. Rudolph Otto, in his great work, *The Kingdom of God and the Son of Man*, says, "Demonism is a phenomenon which moves in waves through history. . . . It may even appear as suddenly as an epidemic." [1] The Bible itself is one evidence for the proof of such waves. In the entire Old Testament there is not a single example of demon possession called by that name.

Steinmeyer points out that in the Gospels the five incidents [2] of healing of those possessed by demons not one occurred in Judea, the center of the theocracy, but always in the extreme borders of Palestine, "partly in heathen countries, partly in those strips of land in Palestine which bordered on a heathen region where the inhabitants dwelt among the heathen, in Galilee of the Gentiles." [3] This observation fits in with the known view that the Jews considered the Gentile world as peculiarly subject to Satan, while they themselves were in a unique way the people of Yahweh. Satan and his demons had no right to possess men made in the image of God. It was one of the great missions of the Messiah to demonstrate his authority over the world of the demonic. Regarding the fact of demon possession C. J. Cadoux has a pertinent observation.

Without forgetting the difference between the imagination of antiquity and scientific evidence, we may observe that there is nothing inherently incredible or improbable in the existence of discarnate beings, who are able to help or harm us in somewhat the same way as our fellow men still living in the flesh are able. Further, there

[1] P. 42.

[2] One is treated in this chapter, and two are treated in the following chapter. The daughter of the Syrophoenician woman and the lunatic boy are discussed in the chapter "Children Jesus Healed."

[3] *Op. cit.*, p. 131.

are certain phenomena in mental disease for which the hypothesis of spirit-possession provides an easier explanation than any other.[4]

In the light of apparently authentic instances from the mission fields of "possession" or domination of one mind by another[5] the modern psychiatrist would distinguish between this form of "demonism" and the psychological condition within a soul which has produced such enormities in our times. The results are tragically the same. Whatever we call it, there is a modern demonism which is rampant in the world today.

There is no point in quibbling over a term in the light of the extermination camps of Dachau, Buchenwald, and the others. No wonder Martin Niemoller could say in an interview with Bishop Bromley Oxnam:

What has been reported is true. Indescribable and incredible things were done. A preacher knows the reason, because he knows sin. These acts were like the practices of sin. A man commits adultery. He is under the conviction of conscience, suffers remorse. But he commits the second act, and conscience does not speak so sharply. And finally he commits adultery without remorse. At first, those ordered to torture and kill did so because they were afraid they would be killed if they did not. Then they became accustomed to brutality, they killed with little feeling, and finally did their terrible work as a matter of routine. The camps were worse than reported. It is like a terrible dream or, worse, the dreaming of a dream within a dream. All is still a nightmare, and you waken to disbelieve today what you know was true just the day before.[6]

It is demonism, pure and simple, that could delight in endeavoring to kill the genius for musical expression that was in Adolf Baller but leave intact all his yearnings to create music. This young Jew had been accompanist for Yehudi Menuhin on many occasions. A virtuoso in his own right, he was on a con-

[4] *Op. cit.,* p. 65. This is especially significant coming from such an outstanding modern scholar, whose views are quite advanced in many fields.

[5] See below, p. 177.

[6] *Christian Century,* June 13, 1945, p. 706.

cert tour in Austria when apprehended by the Gestapo. The sadists among them were not content to starve and beat him, but they trampled his sensitive fingers to a bloody pulp, endeavoring to crush out all of the ability to make glorious melody. Baller, with his hands mangled, finally escaped and made his way back to America. Those who had tried to cripple his genius reckoned without his determination to play once more. After many excruciating hours of exercise and practice he appeared on a program in a little town in California. The musically great of America were there, as well as many leading music critics. A thrill passed through the entire audience as Baller hammered out with power his first number, "The Star-Spangled Banner," with its great crashing chords.

> 'Tis the star-spangled banner; oh, long may it wave,
> O'er the land of the free, and the home of the brave.

Jesus too lived in a demon-filled age. You ask the question, "Did he believe in demons?" The answer is, "Of course he believed in demons." He was too wise not to. Our own generation has been so sophisticated that we have been above believing in demons; but at the very time we proclaim there are no such things, an epidemic of demonism has engulfed us.

One of the busiest days in the ministry of Jesus of which we have a record began with a service of worship in the Capernaum synagogue (Mark 1:21-28; Luke 4:33-37). Jesus, as a well-known itinerant rabbi, was invited to bring the message of the day. Synagogue worship was much less formal in the first century than it is today. Any visiting teacher might be asked to speak or in turn might offer to bring a message or comment upon the Scripture.[7] Consequently Jesus as a rabbi whose fame had spread abroad was often asked to speak. There was something utterly unique and fascinating about his preaching. He did not cite the authorities to bolster his

---

[7] Montefiore, *op. cit.*, I, 32.

message, nor did he use the dramatic introduction of the prophet, "Thus saith the Lord." Rather there was a note of insistent authority in his preaching which can only be termed messianic. "Ye have heard that it was said by them of old time, . . . but I say unto you . . ." (Matt. 5:21-22). No wonder his listeners exclaimed over the remarkable character of his messages as being with authority. In the case we are considering it has been suggested with some degree of insight that the "authority" which astonished the congregation was Jesus' divine sympathy for such an afflicted person. The emphasis in this section is upon the authority of Jesus, which is illustrated here by the casting out of the demon in the synagogue. The authority is underlined by the healing of Peter's mother-in-law, which immediately follows. There was a freshness about the teaching of Jesus which contemporary rabbis lacked. He seemed to his hearers to be fired by the spirit of God. It was an authority of divine inspiration. Dr. Montefiore, in a remarkably fair judgment of the quality of the inspiration of Jesus, said that it was markedly prophetic like that of Amos or Isaiah, but Jesus "does seem to put his own personality more into the forefront than did the prophets. And this personality of his, this personal note, seemed both to claim, and to possess, authority." [8]

During this particular service a man with an unclean spirit—today we would classify him as mentally deranged—evidently becoming excited by the dramatic nature of our Lord's presentation, shouted out, "What have we to do with you, thou Jesus of Nazareth? . . . I know thee who thou art, the Holy One of God." The demon in the man is speaking for his class, hence the use of the plural. There was enough intelligence in his fuddled mind to be aware of the vast gulf between him and the speaker. The recognition of the messianic character of Jesus, *the Holy One of God*, so early in Mark's Gospel has puzzled commentators. The fact that the man who cried out in this fashion was demented or "demon possessed" has added to the difficulty. How-

[8] *Op. cit.,* I, 32.

ever, the situation is not unusual when we reconstruct all of the circumstances. A preacher of such dramatic intensity as to draw from normal persons the exclamation, "He teacheth as one having authority, and not as the scribes," would certainly move a person of excitable temperament. The very lack of inhibitions on the part of such a one, plus the messianic expectancy in the air, is sufficient to account for the incident. Bruce has a startling observation when he says:

*Insanity is much nearer the kingdom of God than worldly-minded-ness.* There was, doubtless, something in the whole aspect and manner of Jesus which was fitted to produce almost instantaneously a deep spiritual impression to which children, simple ingenuous souls like the Galilean fishermen, sinful, yet honest-hearted men like those who met at Matthew's feast, readily surrendered themselves. Men with shattered reason also felt the spell, while the wise and the strong-minded too often used their intellect, under the bias of passion or prejudice, to resist the force of truth.[9]

Dr. Major suggests:

Jesus knew Himself to be the Messiah, and His Messianic Consciousness may have telepathically affected them. Jesus, and this will seem most unexpected, bade them be silent, not because they were demons or because what they said was not true, but because he did not wish to have His Messiahship proclaimed in this way and at this time.[10]

In the days of Jesus demon possession was rampant, because in the thinking of men demons filled the atmosphere. Harnack, in his famous essay, "The Conflict with Demons," [11] demonstrated this clearly.

The whole world and the . . . atmosphere were filled with devils; not merely idolatry, but every phase and form of life was ruled by

[9] *Op. cit.,* p. 187. Italics mine.
[10] Major, Manson, and Wright, *op. cit.,* p. 44.
[11] *Op. cit.,* I, 125-46.

177

them. They sat on thrones, they hovered around cradles, the earth was literally a hell, though it continued to be a creation of God.[12]

In our own day there are many evidences of demonism, as we have seen, but we diagnose the malady in different terms. It is relatively unimportant the name you give to a disease; names vary through the centuries and in different countries, but the symptoms remain the same. Demon possession as an outgrowth of demon belief is psychologically sound. Those who were "possessed" would certainly be influenced by current opinions concerning their malady. Modern missionaries from China, Africa, and the Burma hills report apparently authentic cases of demon possession. This is particularly true in areas in which there is a strong belief in demons as such.

Notice the immediate and remarkable way in which Jesus handled the case before us. As the Messiah, he was to demonstrate his power over all the forces opposed to God's good creation, so he spoke to the demon in the man in dramatically brief but powerful terms, "Be silent, and be gone." It is not the province of this study to go exhaustively into what Jesus actually thought about demon possession. As a man he was a child of his time; but as with so many popular conceptions of his day, such as messianism, his thinking was far in advance of his contemporaries. This was no less true of his view regarding demon possession. Jesus did act as an exorcist, using technical phrases of exorcism, yet at the same time he cast out demons by a word, avoiding carefully the mumbo jumbo of the average exorcist of his period. This was so true that the people remarked, "What new doctrine is this? for with authority commandeth he even the unclean spirits, and they do obey him" (Mark 1:2-7).

We would expect Jesus to use the language of his day. Had he not done so, the record would be suspect. A. C. Headlam observes:

[12] *Ibid.*, p. 131.

Our Lord's language is completely in accordance with the religious and scientific ideas of His contemporaries. He acts recognizing fully what both the onlookers and those whom He cured would think. It is obvious that nothing else would have been possible on His part. . . . A religious teacher who in the first century of the Christian era adopted the scientific language and ideas of the present day would have talked in a language utterly incomprehensible to the people.[13]

Jesus certainly considered one of his primary missions the demonstration of his conquest of Satan by his evidenced power over Satan. Jesus' reputation as an exorcist was of such a character that even in his own lifetime Jewish exorcists had begun to use his name (Mark 9:38). In his own mind this power over demons was clearly one of the proofs of his messianic mission.

The exorcisms, however, do raise the Christological question in another sense, not only because they demonstrate the supernatural power of Christ over the forces of evil, but also because the possession by the demons of superhuman insight enables them to penetrate the mystery, inscrutable to flesh and blood of Who Jesus is.[14]

However, we remember that this particular story occurred quite early in his ministry, and there is the problem we have considered of the recognition of the messiahship of Jesus by one possessed. There is a certain progression in messianic recognition in Mark's Gospel into which this incident fits.[15] It is clear that Jesus did not want messianic recognition by demon-possessed persons; hence his command for silence. Utterances of demoniacs were considered ill-omened and should be discouraged.[16] Only those who are in their right mind are fully capable of un-

---

[13] *The Life and Teaching of Jesus the Christ*, p. 187.

[14] Richardson, *op. cit.*, p. 72.

[15] *Ibid.*, p. 45.

[16] William Manson, *The Gospel of Luke*, p. 46.

derstanding who Jesus is. In time he disclosed himself to his disciples. Messianic understanding does come to those who in faith believe and who have full control of their faculties. God and his Kingdom were never nearer than when Jesus with "the finger of God" demonstrated that he possessed power over demonic forces of all kinds.

# 16

## How Much Better Is a Man

I. THE GERASENE DEMONIAC—*Mark 5:1-20; Matt. 8:28-34;
Luke 8:26-39*

THE MOST dramatic of all incidents of healing a demoniac is
the case of the possessed man of Khersa. The place names in the
three Gospels have given some difficulty where different texts
respectively refer to Gadara, Gerasa, and Gergesa. In all likelihood, the modern town of Khersa on the eastern shore of Galilee
is correctly indentified with the Gergesa of our gospel text, as
this little village fits the general locale of the story. Matthew
refers to two possessed men. He may have conflated this incident
with the one just discussed in the previous chapter, which he
omitted as a separate incident. If one must look for harmony,
Mark and Luke may treat of the more important of the two men.

The accounts give every evidence of violent insanity. The afflicted man is subject to sudden frenzies; he refuses to wear
clothes; the local inhabitants would not give him shelter, so the
poor fellow had to resort to the burial caves in the vicinity.
This added to his own problem, as well as to that of those about
him, for spirits were thought to hover around tombs. A modern
psychiatrist would probably diagnose the case as a schizophrenic
—a man with a split personality. A typical example of this type
of insanity is a person who considers that he is some man of historic greatness, such as Napoleon Bonaparte or Abraham Lincoln. This man was Legion; he was a whole multitude of demons.

Upon leaving the boat in which they had crossed the Sea of

181

Galilee, Jesus and his party were almost immediately espied by the maniac. He at once shouted at Jesus, "What have I to do with thee, Jesus, thou Son of the most high God? I adjure thee by God, that thou torment me not." This latter statement is a reference to the idea that in the age to come demons will be punished.[1] Jesus, with infinite wisdom, demanded the man's name. In that day knowledge of a name was often supposed to give one power over or with a person. This was the reason the ancient Jew hesitated to use the name of God. We get this feeling in the phrase in the Lord's Prayer, "Hallowed be thy name." No wiser method could possibly have been conceived in order to begin a cure in this case. The man replied, "My name is Legion: for we are many"—a quite adequate proof of his split personality. A Roman legion consisted of approximately six thousand soldiers, and this belief that there were many demons within him would add to his mania. Unquestionably the man was influenced by the understanding nature of this conversation with Jesus.

The record continues as if Jesus was conversing with the demons speaking through the demented man. This would be a normal method of telling the story for that day. The demons begged that they not be sent out of the country. One immediately recalls Jesus' statement in Luke 11:24, "When an unclean spirit is gone out of a man, he walketh through dry places, seeking rest; and finding none," an evidence of popular belief about the situation in which demons find themselves without some place of abode. Matthew makes the account specific with a request, "If thou cast us out, suffer us to go away into the herd of swine," which were feeding near by. Matthew then simply has the word "Go," while Mark and Luke say, "He gave them leave."

This whole incident has given an untold amount of difficulty in the past to good folks with conservative economic views—

[1] Enoch 15:6; Jubilees 10:8-9; McNeile, *op. cit.*, p. 112. Compare Philostratus *Life of Apollonius* 4.25: "The phantom pretended to weep and entreated him not to torture it, nor to compel it to declare what it was."

people who lived in days when greater emphasis was put upon property values than today. In the last century Bernhard Weiss met this problem by contending that Jesus did not give permission to enter the swine. He simply used the single word "depart," which does not necessarily express permission.[2] Even if Jesus granted such a request on the part of the demons, the swine's self-destruction did not necessarily have to follow. Many commentators have felt that after Jesus gave the permission, the man himself stampeded the hogs, and they rushed down to the abyss. "The demoniac thereupon rushed on the swine with fury, now playing the part of *agent* for the demons, as before he had played the part of *spokesman*." [3] Richardson has pertinent words of wisdom in connection with the whole account:

If we put out of our minds all modern humanitarian sentiments about kindness to animals, and remember the fixed ideas of the first-century Jews concerning the demons, we shall not imagine that the story is inconsistent with the character of Jesus or devoid of profound spiritual teaching. . . . Jesus performs a thoroughly "humanitarian" act in allowing them to enter the swine.[4]

The healed man wished to become a follower of Jesus but was told instead to go home and tell *his family* what had been done for him. This action is not contrary to the usual injunction of Jesus at this time not to publish abroad cures. The command was, "Tell them how much the Lord [meaning here God] has done for you." If he was a pagan, rather than a Jew, which he could well have been in this locality, the command could be interpreted as a plea to convert his loved ones to a knowledge of the one true God. Some have understood this as a sanction of Jesus for a mission to the Gentiles.

[2] *Op. cit.*, II, 40.

[3] Bruce, *op. cit.*, p. 190. Beyschlag, *op. cit.*, p. 294, also takes this view. I once heard a farmer in answer to this contention say, "Those theologians may know something about the Bible, but they don't know anything about hogs; hogs don't stampede."

[4] *Op. cit.*, p. 73.

What an aftermath there is to the story! Though the former maniac was restored to his right mind and became a flaming evangel of what Jesus had done for him, nevertheless the record tells us that the men of that country asked Jesus to go away! These men were not insane by ancient or modern standards, but they were suffering from a terrible malady that has cursed humanity from the beginning, that of placing property values above human values. They besought the one Man of that day who could have brought them true spiritual understanding to depart from their midst. Contemplate that tragedy for a while! Those of that day believed that demonic forces could destroy animals as well as men. We at least have seen in our generation what happens when men become possessed, and we have also had underlined again the truth that evil is finally self-destructive.

There are many legions of demons still to be driven from our modern civilization; chaos reigns until these demons have been forced out. Their number is legion: war, racial discrimination, economic injustice, ignorance, alcoholism, and that host of personal demons, the lust of the flesh and the pride of life—Christ is adequate to drive them all out.

## II. THE HEALING THAT OCCASIONED THE BEELZEBUB CALUMNY
### —Mark 3:22-30; Matt. 9:32-34; 12:22-32; Luke 11:14-26

Some of the clearest teachings of Jesus regarding demonic forces grow out of the account of his healing another man who was deaf, dumb, and, according to one account in Matthew, blind as well. The cure touched off a bitter accusation against Jesus that he cast out devils by Beelzebub, the prince of devils. The incident itself is brief and would have occasioned little comment had it not been for the charge against Jesus and his defense. Mark's account records no incident of healing, but the fact of a cure is proved by the charges that follow. There is no doubt that a healing took place, or the controversy that grew out of it would be meaningless. Mark's accusation is preceded by a reminiscence that the family of our Lord considered him "beside himself." No wonder Montefiore,[5] following Burkitt,[6] could say, "Here, surely, if anywhere in the gospel, we are listening to the unaltered reminiscences of an eyewitness."

There was a Philistine god of Ekron whose name was Beelzebub. It is spelled variously in different manuscripts. A possible meaning is, "Lord of the heavenly dwelling." However, the Jews, by a slight difference in accent, could give it an offensive meaning, such as "god of dung." It was normal for the monotheistic Jews to degrade the gods of neighboring peoples to the level of demons.    The typical exorcist could cast a demon out only in the name of a power higher than the demon. Sometimes it was in the name of "the most high God." Jewish exorcists cast out demons in the name of Jesus (Mark 9:38). This is a direct and clear evidence of the power he was believed to have possessed, even by those who were not his immediate followers. In our Lord's own exorcism the records do not state that he ever exorcised in the name of another, but he rather used the phrase with the personal pronoun, "I charge thee." As he believed in his own messiahship, this would follow normally and naturally.[7] His enemies, however, made the bitter charge that he was casting out devils in his own name because he himself was the prince of devils, the hated Beelzebub.

We would expect Jesus to react immediately to such a terrible accusation which evidenced the moral perversity of his adversaries in thus calling white, black. To him this was the greatest sin, for it was perversion on a spiritual plane. It becomes the sin against the Holy Spirit—the assertion that good is evil and evil is good. Milton catches this note when he has Satan say, "Evil, be thou my good." With devastating logic and a certain touch of grim irony Jesus asked how Satan could cast out Satan and not destroy his own kingdom? Jesus was not the only exorcist in

[5] *Op. cit.,* I, 91.

[6] *Journal of Theological Studies,* XVII (1915), 11.

[7] For a fuller discussion of Jesus' messianic consciousness, see my *Thinking Where Jesus Thought,* pp. 19 ff.

Palestine, and so he cast in their faces their own charge by saying, "And if I by Beelzebub cast out demons, by whom do your sons cast them out?" The reference to "sons" here is to the Jewish exorcists who could help in certain cases. Jesus believed, as did his accusers, that what power they had was derived from God. His question is then, "Why are not they criticized along with me?" It was as devastating a dilemma for his opponents as his argument about Satan's casting out Satan was irrefutable. The plea is that everyone of intelligence knows that only through goodness is evil defeated. The success of Jewish exorcists was no problem to Jesus. He welcomed all allies in the fight against the demonic. Certainly his "He that is not against us is for us" should be read along with Matt. 12:30 and Luke 11:23. Jesus continues, "But if I with the finger of God [8] cast out devils, no doubt the kingdom of God is come upon you," an evident claim of God's nearness in the person of the Messiah. "God through him is overthrowing the strongholds of Satan. . . . Christ's healings of the possessed have the force of a sign to those who can read them aright." [9] The reign of God is at hand. Here is proof. No neutral attitude toward him is possible. He says that it is all or nothing. "He who is not with me is against me, and he who does not gather with me scatters." (Moffatt.) Yet even as Jesus did his best to keep the allegiance of Judas, so Christ has ever sped with strong feet after the wanderer and even the one who denies. Men from that day to this loudly and blatantly have proclaimed their disbelief in Christ. The English actor Forbes-Robertson tells of a case he witnessed. In his London club there was an atheist by the name of Crow, who constantly and vehemently expressed his disbelief in Christ. This continued until one of the club members posted on the bulletin board the following quatrain:

[8] This expression occurs in Exod. 8:19, "The magicians said unto Pharaoh, This is the finger of God."

[9] Creed, *op. cit.*, pp. 159-60.

We've heard in language highly spiced
That Crow does not believe in Christ,
But what we're more concerned to know
Is whether Christ believes in Crow.

It was answer sufficient, for all knew that this same Christ on the cross had prayed, "Father, forgive them; for they know not what they do."

In Luke's account Jesus continues the discussion of the dispossession of demons. With a remarkable insight into modern psychiatric truth he implies that the place once taken by the demon must be filled with angels, or the devil will return to his original abode and the last state of the man be worse than the first. Modern psychotherapy adds a hearty "Amen" to this. Angels and pixies belong to a child's world, you say, but at least the thing they stand for does have significance. A new comic strip has recently swept the country with a pixy for a hero; Mr. O'Malley is his name, and pink wings are his distinguishing feature! A boon companion of Barnaby, the little boy in the strip, he is not real at all to the lad's parents and their big business friends. The lad knows better, and a lot of adults have been fascinated by Mr. O'Malley's antics. Jesus said, "Except ye . . . become as little children, ye shall in no wise enter into the kingdom of heaven."

In Augustine's life the devil of personal lust was finally swept out. Its place was taken by love for Christ; there is an "angel" indeed to grace any life. Illustrations could be multiplied of those who keep devils out by filling the place with "angels."

Christ died once for all, the just for the unjust, to drive out demons and bring God near to man. The Eternal never came nearer to man than when Jesus with the veritable finger of God defeated on Calvary the greatest of all demons, Satan himself. In George Bernard Shaw's play *Saint Joan* the epilogue poses a soul-stabbing question. It is twenty-five years after Joan, Maid of Orleans, has been burned at the stake. The old rector, now a

187

little daft, recalls what Joan's death did for him. "I did a very cruel thing once, because I did not know what cruelty was like. I had not seen it, you know. That is the great thing: you must see it, and then you are redeemed, and saved!"

To which the bishop replies, "Were not the sufferings of our Lord Jesus Christ enough for you?"

"Oh, no, not all. I had seen them in books and had been greatly moved by them, as I thought. But it was no use. It was not our Lord who redeemed me, but a young woman whom I saw actually burned to death. It was dreadful. But it saved me. I have been a different man ever since."

Then the bishop with pity and scorn put the question our generation must also answer: "Must then a Christ perish in torment in every age to save those who have no imagination?"

Jesus is still adequate to cast out all of our modern demons— personal, national, and international—but men must have sufficient imagination to put their trust in him as the great defeater of demons. It is his ideal of the fatherhood of God and the brotherhood of man which must take the place of the former devils of personal lust, national pride, economic advantage, and racial superiority.

# 17

## The Lord of Life

LIFE situation" is a type of preaching increasingly and justly popular. With it a message grows out of life as it is lived and is pointed toward helping others in similar need. It is one of the oldest of teaching methods. Jesus used it constantly. The greatest speakers have invariably built their messages on life problems and illustrated them with life situations. This was one of the sources of the remarkable pulpit power of Merton Rice. One day he read in the paper about an incubator explosion. Now, an incubator explosion seemed as far from a sermon as one could possibly imagine, but Rice contrasted the mechanical incubator's blowing up with the calmness of a hen, remarking, "Whoever heard of a hen exploding?" From that point he went on to preach a powerful message on the calmness that comes from a vital faith! The Bible is one of the greatest givers of light on life situations. Take for instance the stories of Jairus' daughter and the widow of Nain's son. Here is life as it is lived. There is a vast contrast between the rich and the powerful Jairus, ruler of the synagogue, and the poor widow who was staring destitution in the face. Yet when each was faced with the loss of a beloved child, the reactions were the same.

Those who claim that the gospel records of Jesus' raising persons from the dead are myths usually grant that there is some basis of fact but hold that the story has grown in the telling. The reasoning is somewhat as follows: Jesus of Nazareth was considered a great prophet. As a prophet he had to work this type of miracle, even as Elijah did in the case of the son of the widow at Zarephath (I Kings 17:17-24), and Elisha, when he raised the child of the great woman of Shunem (II Kings 4:32-35). With Jesus a progressive development is claimed. He first raised a little girl, then a youth, then a full-grown man. One was near death; one was dead; and the other had been buried. The Christ of faith has entered the picture, and perforce he must raise the dead.

Whatever one may believe actually took place in these accounts of raising from the dead, the fact remains that Jesus is the great source of the assurance of life. The poets have long sung and the dreamers dreamed about that undiscovered country of man's fondest longings. In our generation Thomas Wolfe has put it:

Something has spoken to me in the night,
Burning the tapers of the waning year;
Something has spoken in the night,
And told me I shall die, I know not where.

Saying:
"To lose the earth you know, for greater knowing;
To lose the life you have, for greater life;
To leave the friends you loved, for greater loving ;
To find a land more kind than home, more large than earth—

"Whereon the pillars of this earth are founded,
Toward which the conscience of the world is tending—
A wind is rising, and the rivers flow." [1]

It is Jesus, however, who has given meaning to immortality. The Egyptians believed in a physical resuscitation; hence with infinite care they embalmed the bodies of their loved ones, wrapping them in hundreds of yards of linen and using many costly unguents and preservatives so that the body might again be able

---

[1] From *You Can't Go Home Again.* Copyright 1940 by Maxwell Perkins, executor. Used by permission Harper & Bros., New York, and William Heinemann, Ltd., London.

THE LORD OF LIFE

to take up its activities in the land beyond death. Many of the pagans longed for immortality. In the days of Jesus the Jews were arguing about it, the Pharisees saying that there is a resurrection, the Sadducees denying it. It was in Jesus that man saw life would really be worth living after death. If he is "the resurrection and the life," we can be satisfied.

I. RAISING THE DAUGHTER OF JAIRUS—*Mark 5:21-43; Matt. 9: 18-26; Luke 8:40-56*

Fairly early in the ministry of Jesus, while he was still preaching and teaching in the lovely land of Galilee, occurred the raising of Jairus' daughter. After restoring to his right mind the lunatic of Gadara or Gerasa, Jesus had been asked to depart by the people of that area. Were they afraid more men would be restored at the cost of more property? In any event, they asked him to leave! He did, for, gentleman that he was, he did not wish to be where he was not wanted. What irony! He left the country of the Gerasenes and immediately thereafter raised the daughter of Jairus, in a neighboring community. In Nazareth "he did not many mighty works there because of their unbelief." His own home town received little benefit from his minstry, because of lack of faith.

Crossing the lake, Jesus landed in Capernaum. Jairus, a ruler of the synagogue, heard that he was back and immediately hastened to him. Ten adult male Jews could organize a synagogue. These became "rulers." [2] They would correspond today somewhat to a cross between a deacon and a trustee in our modern congregations. There is every likelihood that this particular synagogue was built by the wealthy centurion (Luke 7:1-10) who loved the Jewish nation and had built them a house of worship. It is just possible that we have uncovered the ruins of this very synagogue. The mosaics in the floor have all of the pristine beauty and clearness they possessed when they were first laid.

[2] Emil Schurer, *History of the Jewish People in the Time of Jesus Christ*, II, 52-53.

The general opinion is that the ruins are from the second century, yet Klausner thinks they might have been from the first.[3] If so, the feet of Jesus could well have trod upon these very stones.

In the home of Jairus was an only child, a daughter twelve years of age. She was desperately ill, so ill that Jairus knew something must be done or she would be lost. He had gone to the best medical aid the town possessed, but it was not enough. Here is a typical life situation; here is a background for tragedy. Jairus, certainly an intimate friend of the centurion, knew about the remarkable cure Jesus had worked in connection with the centurion's servant.[4] Possibly he could do something for his own daughter, and so he went to find Jesus. According to Mark's Gospel his daughter was not dead when he started out: "My little daughter is at the point of death." Luke tells us, "She lay a dying." Matthew, written considerably later than Mark, has a finality about it, "My daughter has just died." Jairus left home with all of the anguish a father must know under these circumstances, but *he did know where to go for aid*. Jesus was the great resource in time of trouble in that day.

Half the world's ills could be cured if men knew where to go for help. On many occasions we read of sick persons in distant lands being flown to the great medical centers for help they could not receive in their own localities. A Cuban physician brought by air his six-year-old daughter to the University Hospital at Ann Arbor, Michigan, for a delicate brain operation. His child lived because he knew where to go for help. On one occasion the great Scottish surgeon Sir James Simpson was asked, "What is your greatest discovery?" The questioner expected some reply that would deal with his contributions to medicine or surgery. This great scientist, however, replied, "My greatest discovery is that I am a great sinner and that Jesus is a great

[3] See *op. cit.*, p. 262. See also discussion in this volume, p. 124.

[4] Both Matthew and Luke place this incident in the chapter immediately after the account of the centurion's servant, following Q's chronology.

192

Saviour." Christ was and still is the source of help for the needs of men, for the needs of the world. Dr. Harry Emerson Fosdick said, very significantly, on the occasion of his fortieth anniversary as a Christian minister:

Forty years ago, thinking Christians believed that it was necessary to adjust Christ to modern civilization—to modern scientific and intellectual concepts. But today, if the world is to survive, the need is for adjusting modern civilization to Christ. This generation has seen an incredible advance of scientific knowledge, and yet on a scale never known before, ruin is coming to millions upon millions of families around the world. Our knowledge alone cannot save us.

Clement of Alexandria put it long ago, "Jesus changes the sunsets of life into a sunrise."

So Jairus came to Jesus with the anguished prayer of a father about to lose his only daughter. He pleads, "Lay thy hand upon her, and she shall live." Luke tells us that Jesus replied, "She is not dead, but sleepeth." Luke, as a physician, would naturally be interested in the exact physical state of the child. Those who have held to the belief that Jesus in this instance actually raised the little girl from the dead maintain that this statement of Jesus is comparable to that in the incident of Lazarus, where Jesus said, "Lazarus sleepeth." The cases are not quite the same. Though Jesus did use the term "sleep" as referring to death—and it was definitely used that way in the case of Lazarus—he did not say specifically "Lazarus is not dead." We will have to take Jesus at his word here. According to him, the child was not dead.[5] She was in a coma. Modern medical science has never decided just where is the boundary line between life and death. Interesting experiments have been made in draining the blood from the veins of a dog. For a period as long as ten minutes all life apparently ceased, but the blood, kept purified by a special mechanical lung, was then pumped back into the animal, and as the lifeblood

[5] See William Manson, *op. cit.*, p. 99.

returned to its veins, life returned with it. To the fearful father Jesus said, "Fear not: believe only."

The three gospel accounts are ambiguous as to the exact state of the child. They are unanimous that faith in God's power through Christ brought recovery. Such faith will still bring recovery to a needy humanity. We have only begun to plumb the depths of the power of belief. It was a beautiful testimony which Henry Ford gave on his eightieth birthday:

As I look back on my life, the unbroken happiness of my home and the confidence of my wife give me much more personal satisfaction than the building of a world-wide business organization. My wife *believed* in me so much that when many were doubting my early experiments, I called her "The Believer."

The Jewish people in the time of Christ in the semitropical land of Palestine found it necessary to bury their dead within twenty-four hours, and so at the near approach of death preparations would have to be made for the burial. The customary hired mourners must be engaged and every one of the myriad details cared for that were necessary for the last sad rites of those who were deeply loved. When Jesus said, "She is not dead, but sleepeth," the professional mourners naturally laughed him to scorn. They saw their fee evaporating. Jesus took the parents of the little girl, along with Peter, James, and John—that triumvirate who were closest to him and were men of large hearts and deep sympathy. Together they entered the room where the patient lay. Taking the child by the hand, Jesus quietly said, "Little girl, I say to you, arise." It was the expression a happy mother employed to awaken her child in the morning, "Time to get up, little one." Mark recalled the very Aramaic words that he had heard Peter use, *Talitha cumi*. The child responded and sat up. She had been very ill and needed the strength nourishment would give, and so Jesus commanded that food be brought for her. How like Jesus, concerned to the uttermost. After the girl was restored, he was just as thoughtful to see that her strength should be brought back to her. His next word was to enjoin silence. He had difficulty enough in handling the crowds who were thronging him because of his healing. Silence here certainly better served his main purpose.

Many an anguished parent in a similar situation has wished for the physical presence and help of Christ. Yet our generation of Christians has learned the truth John expressed, "It is to your advantage that I go away, for if I do not go away, the Counselor will not come to you" (John 16:7 R.S.V.). John Masefield concludes his drama *The Trial of Jesus* with a dialogue between Pilate's wife and the centurion, followed by the appearance of Jesus himself:

*Pilate's wife:* "Do you think he is dead?"
*Centurion:* "No, lady, I don't."
*Pilate's wife:* "Then, where is he?"
*Centurion:* "Let loose in the world, lady, where neither Roman nor Jew can stop His truth."
*Jesus:*

> Open your hearts, open your mind,
> If ye bind your souls, it is me ye bind;
> Ask of me: seek, and ye shall find;
> Knock, and behold the door shall yield.
> O, brothers, I make the world one kin;
> Open your hearts, and let me in,
> That the reign of my Father may begin
> *And the grave's gates be sealed.*[6]

## II. THE WIDOW'S SON AT NAIN—*Luke 7:11-17*

Nain is perched on a hillside between Gilboa and Shunem, overlooking the fertile Galilean plain of Esdraelon. The only road that leads to the village passes an ancient cemetery. Principal Major, of Oxford, tells us that on a visit to the locality he was much impressed by the accuracy of Luke's account.[7] As

[6] Copyright 1925 by John Masefield. Used by permission the Macmillan Co., publishers.
[7] Major, Manson, and Wright, *op. cit.*, p. 273

PREACHING THE MIRACLES OF JESUS

Jesus approached the town, he met a burial party. It was a typical Eastern funeral of the poor. A young man was carried upon a bier. The only member of a family visible was a woman, but the villagers were all there, trying to make up in their sympathy for the comfort and strength the husband would have given were he living. Jesus sized up the situation at a glance: "And when the Lord saw her," his heart went out to the widow in her need. Notice the term "the Lord." It is peculiarly appropriate to this story. In Mark the title is never used of Jesus on earth, while it is a favorite of Luke. How great compassion belonged to our Lord. He rejoiced with those who rejoiced and wept with those who wept. The record is one of the finest testimonies of the compassion that stirred his heart. Walking over to the bier, Jesus reached out his hand to it, even though this would make him ceremonially "unclean." As in the incident when he touched the lepers to cleanse them, Jesus was far more interested in helpfulness than he was in observing ceremonial minutiae. As he touched the bier, he said, "Young man, I say unto thee, Arise." The one who was carried not only sat up, but began to talk. So far as the record is concerned, it was a restoration to life.[8] As with the previous incident, there is little point in arguing how dead the young man was. Modern medical science might or might not have pronounced him dead. Jesus restored life, but even more, he restored hope in the young man's mother. There would be a consolation and a help for the widow in her old age. All of her dreams and her physical sustenance would not lie cold in the earth. What did Jesus say to the young man? In substance, "Begin to live." Life truly begins, not when we are forty, but

[8] The definiteness of the situation has naturally disturbed radical critics, many of whom dismiss it as completely unhistoric. They see the Elijah-Elisha parallels as a reason for its inclusion in the Gospel. Jesus is shown as mighty, like these worthies. Loisy and others have interpreted the incident symbolically. The disconsolate widow represents Jerusalem, whose only son is recovered through the power of Jesus. Thanks to him, God's promises are not in vain. Montefiore, *op. cit.* (II, 425), feels the story is definitely unhistoric.

when we are genuinely touched by the power of the living Christ.

Physically and spiritually Jesus could and did raise the dead. By men of that day he was considered to have power so to do. He himself even made this clear. When John the Baptist sent from his prison to ask if he was the Messiah, Jesus replied, "Go and shew John again those things which ye do hear and see: the blind receive their sight, and the lame walk, the lepers are cleansed, and the deaf hear, *the dead are raised up*, and the poor have the gospel preached to them" (Matt. 11:4-5). Little do we wonder at the reaction of the people. "They glorified God, saying, *that a great prophet is risen up among us; and, that God hath visited his people.*" Well, God did, and men have never forgotten it, nor shall they.

Dr. Carrol Morong tells of a father in his congregation who came home one night to find his little daughter busily drawing. With fatherly interest he stopped, looked over her shoulder, and asked what she was doing.

Keeping busily at her work, the little girl said, "Drawing."

"I know that, Sweet, but what are you drawing?"

"A picture."

"That is perfectly obvious, but I would like to know what sort of a picture."

"Well, I am drawing a picture of God."

Then tenderly the father said, "Dear, you can't draw a picture of God. No one has ever seen God."

The little girl kept right on with her work as she replied, "Well, they'll see him when I get through."

In a far deeper sense Jesus came to show men God. His one passion in life was to so depict the heavenly Father by his own life that men would never forget.

They have not.

# 18

## Victory at Bethany

THE POETS, no less than the average run of mortals, have been fascinated by what takes place after death. They have been especially intrigued by the story of the raising of Lazarus (John 11:1-53). One recalls Tennyson:

> Where wert thou, brother, those four days?
> There lives no record of reply,
> Which telling what it is to die
> Has surely added praise to praise.[1]

John's account of what took place at Bethany in the raising of Lazarus (11:1-53) presents the whole problem of miracle in its most acute form. This is especially so if the literal, rather than the symbolic, is stressed. We began our study of the miracles of Jesus with John's record of turning the water into wine. "This beginning of miracles did Jesus." It is as well to end our study with the restoration of life to Lazarus. John's seven "signs" by which he summed up and typified the mighty works of Jesus began with Cana and ended with Bethany. As he himself explained, his purpose was to establish that Jesus was the Christ, sent from the Father with power from on high. It is true that the raising of Lazarus is one of three such instances recorded in the Gospels, yet the question of whether death had actually taken place must be considered with the stories of Jairus' daughter and of the widow of Nain's son. The record as we have it is clearly designed to show that there can be absolutely

[1] *In Memoriam,* XXXI.

no question about the death of Lazarus. He was not only dead, but had been buried for four days. Even though the account stresses that death as we know it had taken place, the question is still pertinent, When does restoration become impossible? There are many instances of medical resuscitation which almost take on the nature of miracle. A. E. Garvie remarks, "Do we know enough about what death involves as regards the relation of soul and body to be able to say when, if restoration be at all possible, it becomes impossible?"[2]

It might be well to keep in mind the matter of degrees in miracle. When one considers the problem at all thoughtfully, it is soon recognized that one genuine miracle is not more wonderful than another. Only from the human standpoint does this seem to be the case.[3] In the past apologists have contended that the accounts of the walking on the water and the raising of Lazarus are supreme proofs of the divine power of Jesus. They are utilizing a false premise no less than the rationalist who attacks just these miracles as being supremely improbable. If miracle as we have defined it in Chapter 1 has ever taken place or ever does take place, then the problem of greater or lesser degree is completely irrelevant.

A far more pertinent problem is: Why is this very remarkable incident recorded only by John? Other striking events, such as the triumphant entry or the cleansing of the temple, are mentioned by all four Gospels. John makes it his *cause célèbre* which precipitated the crucifixion. The generally accepted view is that John was not following the actual chronology of the life of Jesus when he placed the incident of cleansing the temple at the beginning of the public ministry. It served John's purpose of a striking inaugural act with which to begin the career of the Messiah. In John's scheme a dramatic incident was necessary to lead up

[2] *Abingdon Bible Commentary*, p. 1080.
[3] See Shafto, *op. cit.*, p. 173.

to the trial and death of Jesus, and in "his sources, which were partly independent of the Synoptic tradition," [4] he found the Lazarus story. It fitted his purpose perfectly, and he used it with telling effect. The argument that if the event had actually taken place, the synoptic writers certainly would have recorded it is very strong and cannot be set aside lightly. However, there was no Associated Press in that day, and photographic exactness is not to be expected. We have only fragments of the story at best. Furthermore, silence is an argument, but never a conclusive one. Only Luke tells the story of the prodigal son.

New Testament criticism is coming increasingly to the conviction that Peter and John furnish the two main sources for our knowledge of the life of Jesus. The Synoptics, our first three Gospels, depend to a large extent on Peter's reminiscences which we find in Mark's Gospel. New Testament scholars generally accept as accurate the statement of the early-church father Papias:

And the presbyter said this. Mark, having become the interpreter of Peter, wrote down accurately whatsoever he remembered. It was not, however, in exact order that he related the sayings or deeds of Christ. For he neither heard the Lord nor accompanied Him. But afterward, as I said, he accompanied Peter, who accommodated his instructions to the necessities [of his hearers], but with no intention of giving a regular narrative of the Lord's sayings. Wherefore Mark made no mistake in thus writing some things as he remembered them. For of one thing he took especial care, not to omit anything he had heard, and not to put anything fictitious into the statements.[5]

There are a number of other sources that scholars recognize, such as Q—also known as the Logia or Sayings of Jesus—Matthew's special material designated as M, and Luke's special material designated as L. However, the framework for the first three Gospels is that of Mark, *and he is dependent upon Peter.*

---

[4] Strachan, *op. cit.*, p. 226.
[5] Fragment VI. *The Ante-Nicene Fathers*, I, 154-55 (Edinburgh ed.).

John's Gospel is gaining recognition as an accurate and valuable source for our knowledge about the life of Jesus.[6] Dr. A. T. Olmstead, of the University of Chicago, in his highly significant *Jesus in the Light of History* maintains that John published his memoirs of Jesus very shortly after the crucifixion, his principal proof being John 7:41-43, in which the enemies of Jesus object to the recognition that he is the Messiah. "Is the Christ to come from Galilee? Has not the scripture said that the Christ is descended from David, and comes from Bethlehem, the village where David was?" The argument is that later stories say that Jesus was born at Bethlehem, but that when John wrote all the information he had was that Jesus was a Galilean. Dr. Olmstead says this Gospel was written less than ten years after the tragedy of the crucifixion.[7] He places large reliance upon John's Gospel as being an extremely accurate account of what took place. It is certain that the Synoptic Gospels do not show the intimate knowledge of the Jerusalem situation which we find in John.[8] Though W. F. Albright does not hold to the historical value of John as compared with the Synoptics, he does say:

One is quite justified in maintaining that it [John] does reflect a side of Jesus which was too mystical for the ordinary man of that date to understand and which he presumably held in reserve for a few intimates.[9]

Ernest Findlay Scott can write:

Nothing could be further from the truth than the assertion so often made that in the Fourth Gospel the real Jesus disappears, and gives place to an imaginary being—a divinity disguised for a brief

[6] It is not a part of this work to discuss the highly intricate and technical problem connected with the authorship of John's Gospel.

[7] *Op. cit.*, pp. 256, 244. I do not accept this extreme view but have quoted it to show that the question is not a closed one.

[8] See John 11:47-57, especially verse 53.

[9] *From the Stone Age to Christianity*, p. 299.

time in human form. It was for the very purpose of refuting such a doctrine that John wrote his Gospel.[10]

Inasmuch as we do not have an account of the raising of Lazarus in the Synoptic Gospels, a conjecture as to the reason for this is in order: It is entirely likely that Peter was not present in Perea or later at Bethany. When Jesus remarked that they must return to Bethany, Thomas is specifically mentioned in the account as saying to his fellow disciples, "Let us also go, that we may die with him" (John 11:16). He is apparently acting as the spokesman for the group, *a role that in every other instance Peter occupies.* If Peter had been with Jesus and the disciples in Perea, from what we know of the man he would surely have spoken up, and it most certainly would have been recorded.[11] If John's Gospel is very late, written long after the Synoptics, as the great majority of scholars hold, it would be natural for the incident about Lazarus not to appear in the earlier Gospels. Were Lazarus alive at the time the Synoptics were written, he would be constantly bothered by curious folks wanting to know what took place, even if his life would not have been in jeopardy. At the time John wrote, according to this view, he would be free to tell the story, for Lazarus had long since passed on. The Fourth Gospel in a number of places supplements the Synoptics.

Some modern students make the whole story of the raising of Lazarus a dramatic allegory [12] which grew out of hints found in the first three Gospels. Putting together the raising of Jairus' daughter, the Nain widow's son, the story of Mary and Martha, plus the parable of the rich man and Lazarus, which ends with the statement, "Neither will they be persuaded, though one rose from the dead," some scholars have found sufficient material for a poetic and allegorical mind to construct the account of the raising of Lazarus. John is allegorical, and he does write with a

---

[10] *The New Testament Idea of Revelation,* p. 186.

[11] Bernard, *op. cit.,* II, 381.

[12] Major, Manson, and Wright, *op. cit.,* pp. 844-50.

purpose, as he says, but a completely allegorical interpretation is always fraught with danger and leads to most fanciful extremes.[13] Wright, who holds that the best interpretation for our day is allegorical, nevertheless warns that it is sheer blindness to say that the scene is either an imposture or fiction; it is rather a parable of the spiritual mission of Jesus.[14] After all, is there not some wisdom for us in the position of Augustine and the church fathers who held to the literal facts and yet at the same time drew an allegorical lesson, maintaining that there were two meanings in all such passages, the literal and the spiritual?

We now know and accept that the truest history has to pass through the mind of the writer and that it is not *less true* for so exhibiting the author's reaction to the events described, but *more true*. There is literary artistry in John 11, but factual reality is also there. Whatever may have been Sanday's later views, his observation is still pertinent that the evangelist inventing this story would be a literary marvel "more difficult to accept than the miracle." [15] Dr. Olmstead, in speaking of the incident, remarks:

Such is the story originally told by John and with all the circumstantial detail of the convinced eyewitness. It is utterly alien in form to the literary miracle tale. As with so many accounts found in our best sources, the historian can only repeat it, without seeking for psychological or other explanations.[16]

A. E. Garvie says that it is "a narrative that for the most part can claim historical probability in its main features." [17] Strachan, who has done careful work on John, says that to treat it as pure fact is to turn poetry, the highest form of truth, into prose, but

[13] See Macgregor, *op. cit.*, p. 253; also Bernard, *op. cit.*, II, 382. The latter calls much of the allegorizing of modern scholars "fantastic."

[14] Major, Manson, and Wright, *op. cit.*, p. 833.

[15] Quoted in Shafto, *op. cit.*, pp. 163-64.

[16] *Op. cit.*, p. 206.

[17] *Op. cit.*, p. 1081.

at the same time he acknowledges, "There can be no doubt that underlying it is a substratum of historic fact." [18]

Here we have a picture of a very human Jesus. He is moved by human emotions; he cannot restrain his tears in a genuine expression of sympathy. He asks the place of burial, as would any normal man. He wants to know the will of his heavenly Father. He prays a human prayer and acts in obedience to what he believes is the will of God. Here is no Docetic phantasm but a true-to-life portrait of the same type of Person we find in the first three Gospels. In the sequel to the story in John 12 there is the same normal reaction which we would expect to such a story. A great crowd of people gathered, not to see Jesus this time, but "that they might see Lazarus also" (vs. 9). To this is added a consideration by the chief priests of the necessity for putting Lazarus to death, "because that by reason of him many of the Jews went away, and believed on Jesus." These men are in character too. Such natural vividness is held to be the mark of historic truth in other narratives; it cannot be less here.

John makes the incident one of those which helped to precipitate the crisis that brought about the crucifixion of Jesus. His placing of it here as an introduction to the Passion could well have been his way of making the same assertion concerning the messiahship of Jesus that the Synoptic Gospels do in the Caesarea-Philippi narrative. *Jesus in this final "sign" believes that as the Messiah he is completely in the will of God, even to bringing Lazarus back from the grave.*

No understanding of the life of Jesus is complete that does not take into very vital account his messianic concept. From the very beginning the Nazarene faced the problem of what sort of Messiah he would be. John Wick Bowman, in a remarkable study, *The Intention of Jesus*, expounds brilliantly the thesis that Jesus presented himself as the Messiah of the Remnant who was the Suffering Servant of Deutero-Isaiah. No wonder Walter

[18] *Op. cit.,* p. 225.

Horton could say of this book, [It] is the most credible speaking likeness of the real Jesus that I have ever encountered." [19] This position, of course, has been advanced before. James Moffatt wrote, "[Jesus] regarded himself as in the world to carry out such a vocation as that which had been attributed to the Suffering Servant of God in the later Judaism—in a passage which connects his death with human sin as in some way a vicarious offering." [20] C. H. Dodd remarks, "The phenomenon of a 'crucified Messiah' was a scandal to the Jews. It could not have come from anywhere except out of history." [21] At the very beginning of Jesus' ministry the temptations of Satan were temptations concerning his messianic status. The record says, "And when the devil had ended all the temptation, he departed from him for a season" (Luke 4:13). The question of his messianic relation must have kept recurring to him. At Caesarea-Philippi, Jesus brought the question into the open by asking the disciples specifically who he was.

Jesus' high conception of the work of the Messiah is seen under the following heads: (1) *It is spiritual.* "Man shall not live by bread alone." (Luke 4:4.) (2) *It is moral.* "Lord, . . . if I have taken any thing from any man by false accusation, I restore him fourfold." (Luke 19:8.) The moral demands of Jesus were so evident that Zacchaeus caught them at once. We see this also in the parable of the good Samaritan. (3) *It is universal.* "Wheresoever this gospel shall be preached throughout the whole world, this also that she hath done shall be spoken of for a memorial of her." (Mark 14:9.) (4) *It is redemptive.* "Thy sins be forgiven thee." (Mark 2:5.) (5) *It is life-giving.* "I am the resurrection, and the life." (John 11:25.)

There is no attempt in the above to work out an ascending order, but the task of giving eternal life to men with all that it implies certainly sums up the other factors in Jesus' messianic

[19] From the Foreword, p. vii.
[20] *The Approach to the New Testament,* p. 93.
[21] *History and the Gospel,* p. 67.

concept. In Hebrew theology death came into the world as a result of sin, as man's punishment for his disobedience to God. Jesus said that he had come to give men life, and that more abundantly (John 10:10). Is it too much to believe that the incident of the raising of Lazarus comes as a final and complete vindication in his own heart of the correctness of his life and ministry? If God would hear him in the raising of Lazarus, then the result of his own coming death on the cross would not be in doubt in his own heart. There would be, nonetheless, shrinking from the ordeal, the humiliation and the suffering of the cross, but Jesus at least would know beyond the peradventure of a doubt that he had not led his disciples along a false path, that he was the resurrection and the life. This view would tend to account for the real difficulties which we find in connection with verses 4 and 15, which otherwise strike the reader as overdramatic and entirely too much influenced by the succeeding events.

Bethany was two miles from Jerusalem. There lived a family Jesus dearly loved. The figures of Mary and Martha are in complete character. The two sisters are the women of Luke's narrative (10:38-42). The complete veracity with which each figure is drawn is a strong guarantee for the genuineness of the author's sources. True, the figure of Lazarus is hazy, but this is to be expected in the passive role he played. The messenger does say of him, "Behold, he whom thou lovest is sick." Interestingly enough, the only other one so designated in the Gospels is the rich young ruler. It seems to me that it would have been well-nigh impossible for a literary artist of the first century to have written the account so completely in keeping with what we know of the various figures had he not been there in person and had he not possessed, himself, somewhat of the mystical nature that must have belonged to Jesus. It was a nature which could tie closely the world of the eternal with the world of the contemporary.

In the household the brother, Lazarus, fell ill. A messenger was immediately dispatched to Jesus with the news of the sickness. Jesus said to the disciples, when he heard the news, "This sickness is not unto death, but for the glory of God, that the Son of God might be glorified thereby." This strange verse has caused no end of trouble to Bible students. The words "this sickness is not unto death" may have some ultimate bearing on how the event took place. We shall consider it shortly. Jesus delayed purposely for two days. John apparently makes the situation more theatrical than was warranted. It would be hard to believe that Jesus delayed so that his friend might die. Jesus was simply tarrying, waiting for divine guidance from his heavenly Father.[22]

There was danger at Bethany. It was just two miles from Jerusalem, the general headquarters of those who were seeking to destroy him. Shortly prior to this Jesus and his disciples had been forced to flee Jerusalem and environs. The disciples pointed out that they had sought to stone him there, and asked if he really intended to return. When they saw that he was completely determined to go in response to the call for help, with despairing loyalty Thomas cried out to his brethren, "Let us also go, that we may die with him." How plain and how powerful is this dramatic lesson that Jesus is teaching by his actions. He always goes where there is human need. "Are there not twelve hours in the day?" We can continue in a paraphrase, "While we live, must we not do good? Walk in the light no matter what the cost." So Jesus ventured into the danger zone of Jerusalem to help his friend. He himself said, "Greater love hath no man than this, that a man lay down his life for his friends" (John 15:13). Could he do less than risk a visit to one whom he dearly loved? The Christian Church has rightfully recognized that Jesus ever comes to human need. If he comes to human need, so ought his followers to go even into the jaws of death itself in order to bring succor to a suffering, anxious, and helpless humanity. We have the assurance that the Lord will be with us. Significantly enough, John continues his narrative in the twelfth chapter with the

[22] So Macgregor, *op. cit.*, p. 246, and many others.

207

story of Mary's anointing. Here the author is saying that Mary, with overwhelming gratitude, had realized that in giving life to Lazarus, Jesus had laid down his own life.

How vividly John pictures the home where death has entered. The townsmen are there to comfort the sisters. Characteristically the pensive Mary, bowed down with grief, sits and waits for Jesus to come, while Martha rushes out to meet him and, frantically almost, chides him, "If you had been here, my brother would not have died." Mary later uses the same words. His power and willingness to help are clear to both. Martha continued, "Whatever you ask from God, God will give you." This is no expectation of a restoration to life, as verse 24, with its recognition that the brother would rise in the last day, shows. The heart of the whole account is found in the dramatic words of Jesus, "I am the resurrection and the life; he who believes in me, though he die, yet shall he live, and whosoever lives and believes in me shall never die." Martha's thoughts are turned from distant resurrection, which is all too remote to give comfort in the present situation, to the glorious fact of the resurrection of which Jesus is both source and agent.[23] In this passage, with supreme ability Jesus turned the mind from an everlasting future "in the resurrection" to a glorious and eternal now; "I *am* the resurrection and the life."

The life which Christ bestows is based on a *personal relation*. No matter what might be one's physical state—"though he die" —yet "shall he live."

In the Fourth Gospel Jesus is the Water, the Bread, the Light, the Door, the Shepherd, the Vine, the Way, the Truth, the Life. Because he is the Life, even in face of mortal death, he is the Resurrection.

No one can give what he has not got. Jesus gives this life to men because He has it. And those who have it "shall never die." Just as the Gospel has been saying repeatedly that men are "judged" *now*,

[23] Bernard, *op. cit.*, II, 387.

so this passage says that the "resurrection" is *now*. It is *now* or *never:* and because it is *now*, it is *ever.* All the figures which Jesus uses of Himself are figures to express not a temporal or future reality, but an *eternal* reality. He is "water," and water quenches man's thirst *now:* He is bread, and bread feeds *now.* Stagnant water is not the water of life. Bread that is left unused is not the bread of life. Thus Jesus is "resurrection and life" *now.* Men speculate about a future day which they have called the day of the "general resurrection." What Jesus says is that the coming to life should be *here* and *now*, and that the life which thus comes transcends the dissolution of what we call *matter*, and the passage of what we call *time.*[24]

The scholar in his cell can say that John 11 is dramatic allegory. The pastor who has brought comfort in many such homes where death has breathed upon a loved form and all is still, knows that it is life and it is real. Martha's faith and Mary's faith are joined by the faith of the mourners in the remarkable power of Jesus. "Could not this man, which opened the eyes of the blind, have caused that even this man should not have died?" (11:37). *Neither Mary, Martha, nor the crowd expected that Lazarus would come back from the dead.* One cannot escape the feeling that if this story had been invented around the first century, with the high Christological views then held, the faith of the two sisters, plus that of the mourners, would have been represented in far more positive terms. They would have expected a resurrection. The account as it now stands gives simply the expectation that Jesus as a mighty worker could have prevented death. The shortest verse in the entire Bible now follows, "Jesus wept." The human sympathy of our Lord overflowed, and he wept with the others in their sorrow. The artlessness of this account is surpassed only by the artlessness exhibited in the accounts of his own crucifixion and resurrection.

When they came to the tomb, Jesus ordered the stone removed. Martha reminded him, "He hath been dead four days."

---

[24] Major, Manson, and Wright, *op. cit.*, p. 843.

These four days are significant. As we have seen, in Palestine burial was on the same day as death. As the custom was to bury in caves in the hillside for the most part, it is clear that there would be an occasional record of a resuscitation, in which a supposedly-dead person would be revived by the cool of the tomb. Consequently, the custom developed of the family's visiting the tomb for *three* days, hoping against hope. Likewise, the Jews believed that the spirit hovered about the body for this length of time until the countenance changed. Martha also said, "He stinketh." Her opinion was that decomposition had set in because of the length of time elapsed. If we now tie up verse 4, where Jesus said, "This sickness is not unto death, but for the glory of God," with verse 15, "I am glad for your sakes that I was not there," and verse 40, "Jesus saith unto her, Said I not unto thee that, if thou wouldst believe, thou shouldest see the glory of God?" we may begin to have a *modus operandi* for the miracle, if we need such. In verse 41 there is the prayer of Jesus, "Father, I thank thee that thou *hast* [25] heard me." Is this not evidence that Jesus had been praying, possibly from the time when he first heard of the illness in Perea, and that his prayers, plus a conviction that God would work through him a mighty deed, were sufficient to preserve the body of Lazarus in some state corresponding to that of suspended animation?

After the prayer of thanksgiving, spoken as if Lazarus had already been restored, there is the difficult statement, "I have said this on account of his people standing by." The latter part of the prayer seems highly artificial. However, it is typically Johannine and is his way of saying that Jesus always wanted the people to know that the source of his spiritual and moral power was God.

Jesus then cried, "Lazarus, come forth." Lazarus heard the voice and obeyed the imperious command of the Lord of life

[25] ἤκουσάς (aorist past tense).

and walked out of the tomb, with the graveclothes wrapped about him.[26] G. K. Chesterton dramatically puts it:

> After one moment when I bowed my head
> And the whole world turned over and came upright
> And I came out where the old road shone white,
> I walked the ways and heard what all men said. . . .
> The sages have a hundred maps to give
> That trace their crawling cosmos like a tree,
> They rattle reason out through many a sieve
> That stores the sand and lets the gold go free:
> And all these things are less than dust to me
> Because my name is Lazarus and I live.[27]

John brings the story to a conclusion here. Except for the reaction of those who seeing believed, and others who seeing recognized that from their standpoint Jesus was a very dangerous individual to have on the loose, the account ends. This is perplexing to some, yet to those who read John aright it is consummate art, as Loisy well saw: "The absence of a conclusion invites the reader to raise himself heavenwards and seek among the celestial verities for that last word which the story seems to lack."[28] In our mind's eye we can continue the story as Mary and Martha took their brother Lazarus by the hand and led him home. They had seen the glory of God in the face of Jesus, their friend and house guest. Jesus too had seen the glory of his heavenly Father in the answer to his prayer. The assurance in his own heart was complete. He could face his coming passion with the knowledge that even through the suffering and the travail which apparently would darken for a moment his relationship with his Father in the tragic cry, "Why hast thou for-

[26] Quibbles about how a man wrapped in graveclothes could walk are not pertinent. The limbs could have been wrapped separately, or some movement would be possible with the tightest wrapping.

[27] "The Convert" from *Collected Poems of G. K. Chesterton,* copyright 1911 by Dodd, Mead & Co. Used by permission of Dodd, Mead & Co., New York, Methuen & Co., London, and the author's executrix.

[28] Quoted in Macgregor, *op. cit.,* p. 253.

saken me?" there would come the final assurance as he could say to his dear Father, "Into thy hands I commend my spirit."

Martha had expressed the dim, distant faith of meeting Lazarus again in the resurrection. Jesus, with words that have sung themselves into the faith of countless generations, replied, "I am the resurrection, and the life: he that believeth in me, though he were dead, yet shall he live; and whosoever liveth and believeth in me shall never die." "The resurrection and the life." Here we have the last and the greatest of John's magnificent series of metaphors. Jesus is the incarnate Word, the Lamb of God, the Light of the World, the Good Shepherd. Above all, he is the Resurrection and the Life. Jesus is the Lord of life and love. For the Christian, death is not what it seems. Those who believe in Christ are not dead. A living Lazarus is the proof. Of Jesus we instinctively feel that his category of existence was such that he, of all men, deserved to live. Man that he was—and along with the Early Church we must hold this with the utmost vigor—still Christian faith from the beginning has seen in Jesus a uniqueness that could be explained only in terms of such close relationship to God that he becomes one with God. As such Jesus could not "be holden of death." But Lazarus was a man even as you and I. His living at the call of the Galilean is superb witness that Jesus is the resurrection and the life.

> The very God! think, Abib; dost thou think?
> So, the All-Great, were the All-Loving too—
> So, through the thunder comes a human voice
> Saying, "O heart I made, a heart beats here!
> Face, my hands fashioned, see it in myself!
> Thou hast no power nor mayst conceive of mine,
> But love I gave thee, with myself to love,
> And thou must love me who have died for thee!"
> [Lazarus] saith He said so: it is strange.[29]

[29] Robert Browning, "Karshish."

212

# Bibliography

No ATTEMPT can be made here to survey exhaustively the modern field of works on miracles. Specific volumes in English in the last hundred years began with R. C. Trench's large work, *Notes on the Miracles of Our Lord* (1855), in which miracles were simply accepted. We then enter a period of apologetics with J. B. Mozley's *On Miracles* (1872) and A. B. Bruce's *The Miraculous Element in the Gospels* (1886). This period might be said to have come to an end with Johannes Wendland's *Miracles and Christianity* (1911). About this time J. M. Thompson published *Miracles in the New Testament*, in which he took a highly critical view of gospel miracles. His book occasioned a fresh outburst of publication, both in reviews and in books. William Adams Brown wrote his essay "The Permanent Significance of Miracles for Religion" in the *Harvard Theological Review*, July, 1915. However, materialistic and modernistic views were forging ahead. Miracle as such continued to be in disrepute.

A general discussion began again late in the twenties. By 1929 E. R. Micklem had written his *Miracles and the New Psychology;* F. R. Tennant, *Miracle and Its Philosophical Presumptions;* and C. J. Wright, *Miracle in History and in Modern Thought*. The latter is the outstanding large work that covers the whole field.

A revived interest in the whole question has grown in very recent days, beginning with Alan Richardson's *Miracle Stories of the Gospels* (1942). In this he treats the gospel miracles with high scholarship and genuine Christian understanding. Most recently C. S. Lewis has gone into the whole philosophy behind miracle for the modern Christian in his outstanding book *Miracles* (1947).

The following list contains the major works dealing with the problem of miracles, arranged in approximate chronological order of publication. The second section contains books of special homiletic value.

## I. GENERAL

Hume, David. *An Enquiry Concerning the Human Understanding.* 1747. Chapter 10.
> A classic essay that marked the beginning of the modern discussion of the whole miracle problem.

Campbell, George. *Dissertation on Miracles.* 1763.
> A long refutation of Hume's position.

Trench, Richard C. *Notes on the Miracles of Our Lord.* New York: D. Appleton & Co., 1855.
> The famous standard work on the gospel miracles, taking them up individually. Invaluable for patristic information, as well as for views of older critical scholars.

Hovey, Alvah. *The Miracles of Christ*. Boston: Graves & Young, 1864.
Traditional discussion by a president of Newton Theological Institution.

Mozley, J. B. *On Miracles*. London: Rivingtons, 1867.
The Bampton lectures. A classic apologetic for miracle from the traditional viewpoint.

Steinmeyer, F. L. *The Miracles of Our Lord*. Edinburgh: T. & T. Clark, 1875.
"Does not attempt to explain the miracles, but takes the broad ground of the omnipotence of God, which no theist can deny, and then shows the probability of Jesus having performed miracles."

Bruce, Alexander B. *The Miraculous Elements in the Gospels*. London: Hodder & Stoughton, 1886.
Although the date is 1886, and in general the position is traditional, this study can well be called the first of the modern treatments of the gospel miracles. There is a mine of valuable help. Scholarly and thorough.

Wendland, Johannes. *Miracles and Christianity*. London: Hodder & Stoughton, 1911.
A thoughtful apologetic for the miracle concept by a German scholar. The last of the major works in this general period. "In Jesus God has spoken His final word. . . . We would expect Him to work miracles." Translated by H. R. Mackintosh, who says of it, "I think we need his teaching that faith in miracle is faith in a living God."

Gordon, George A. *Religion and Miracle*. Boston: Houghton Mifflin Co., 1910.
Nathaniel Taylor lectures at Yale by former pastor of Old South Church, Boston. "I am concerned to show that where miracle has ceased to be regarded as true, Christianity remains in its essence entire."

Thompson, James M. *Miracles in the New Testament*. London: Arnold Co., 1911.
A highly critical view of the gospel miracles. Gave utterance to the pent-up feeling of the whole liberal school. Scholarly, but dogmatic.

Headland, A. C.; Holland, H. S.; Lock, W.; Sanday, W.; and Williams, H. N. *Miracles*. New York: Longmans, Green Co., 1911.
Series of papers in answer to Thompson's book. An indication of the intense interest aroused at this time.

Davies, E. O. *Miracles of Jesus*. London: Hodder & Stoughton, 1913.
Traditional view argumentatively presented. Helpful.

Headlam, Arthur C. *The Miracles of the New Testament*. London: John Murray, 1914.
Moorhouse lectureship. Historical review. Presentation of reasoned basis for belief in gospel miracles by high-grade New Testament scholar.

Fonck, L. *I Miracoli del Signore*. Rome, 1914.
Exhaustive work in Italian, "with the approval of church authorities."

Brown, William Adams. "Permanent Significance of Miracles for Religion," *Harvard Theological Review*, July, 1915.
An effort to maintain the significance of miracle concept for Christian faith.

————. *God at Work*. New York: Charles Scribner's Sons, 1933.
A further expansion of the above theme by a first-rate thinker and churchman. Typical of the newer approach to the problem. "A re-interpretation of the supernatural factor in religion, not from the abstract and theoretical

viewpoint which has been controlling in many recent discussions of the subject, but in its bearing upon the personal religious life."

Illingworth, John R. *Gospel Miracles*. New York: The Macmillan Co., 1915.
"An attempt to vindicate the occurrence of the gospel miracles as being intrinsically congruous with the Incarnation, considered as the great enfranchisement of human life by its deliveries from the slavery to sin." Virgin birth, resurrection, and prayer discussed. Final chapter: "Miracles and Modern Thought."

Micklem, Edward R. *Miracles and the New Psychology*. London: Oxford University Press, 1922.
A scholarly presentation based on the insights that modern psychology gives.

Tennant, F. R. *Miracle and Its Philosophical Presupposition*. New York: The Macmillan Co., 1926.
A highly philosophical but important consideration of the problems involved for the modern thinker.

Fridrichsen, A. *Le Problème du Miracle*. Strasbourg, 1925.
Doctor's dissertation on the miracle problem in the light of primitive Christianity.

Case, Shirley Jackson. *Experience with the Supernatural in Early Christian Times*. New York: Century Co., 1929.
Sound historical study by an advanced but careful thinker.

Wright, Charles J. *Miracle in History and in Modern Thought*. New York: Henry Holt & Co., 1930.
A leading English New Testament scholar writes the outstanding work in the whole field. No consideration is overlooked. The position is critical of traditional views, but sympathetic to the religious problems involved.

Box, H. S. *Miracles and Critics*. Milwaukee: Morehouse-Goreham Co., 1935.
A good modern apologetic.

Rogers, C. F. *The Case for Miracle*. New York: The Macmillan Co., 1936.
Deals largely with resurrection and virgin birth. Based on open-air discussions. Scholarly.

Richardson, Alan. *The Miracle-Stories of the Gospels*. New York: Harper & Bros., 1942.
The finest modern critical study of the gospel miracles. The author combines high scholarship and the latest in New Testament research to support the genuine values that underlie the miracle stories. He makes a powerful case for compassion as a motive for the miracles.

Lewis, C. S. *Miracles*. New York: The Macmillan Co., 1947.
A major philosophical apologetic by the keen Oxford don who has done so much to present to the average man the philosophical and theological truths of Christianity. Written in his own inimitable style.

II. HOMILETIC

Westcott, B. F. *Gospel Miracles*. New York: The Macmillan Co., 1859.
Scholarly sermons. Typical of mid-nineteenth century.

Howland, J. S. *Meditations on the Miracles*. London: Religious Tract Society, 1861.

Taylor, William M. *The Miracles of Our Saviour*. New York: Harper & Bros., 1928.

A homiletical treatment with some help.

Lang, Cosmo Gordon. *The Miracles of Jesus*. New York: E. P. Dutton & Co., 1910.

Messages that grew out of the miracles. Neither apologetic nor critical, yet went through twelve editions. Delightful style, helpful to the student and preacher.

Shafto, G. R. H. *The Wonders of the Kingdom*. New York: George H. Doran Co., 1924.

A discussion of the miracles of Jesus with emphasis upon their preaching values. "Written for the Student Christian Movement to meet the need for a concise work on the miracles of Jesus."

Douglas, Lloyd C. *Those Disturbing Miracles*. New York: Harper & Bros., 1927.

# Index of Scripture References

# Index of Subjects